teach yourself®

portuguese phrasebook
sue tyson-ward

For over sixty years, more than 40 million people have learnt over 750 subjects the **teach yourself** way, with impressive results.

be where you want to be
with **teach yourself**

For UK order enquiries: please contact Bookpoint Ltd, 130 Milton Park, Abingdon, Oxon OX14 4SB. Telephone: +44 (0)1235 827720. Fax: +44 (0)1235 400454. Lines are open 09.00–18.00, Monday to Saturday, with a 24-hour message answering service. Details about our titles and how to order are available at www.teachyourself.co.uk

For USA order enquiries: please contact McGraw-Hill Customer Services, PO Box 545, Blacklick, OH 43004-0545, USA. Telephone: 1-800-722-4726. Fax: 1-614-755-5645.

For Canada order enquiries: please contact McGraw-Hill Ryerson Ltd, 300 Water St, Whitby, Ontario L1N 9B6, Canada. Telephone: 905 430 5000. Fax: 905 430 5020.

Long renowned as the authoritative source for self-guided learning – with more than 30 million copies sold worldwide – the **teach yourself** series includes over 300 titles in the fields of languages, crafts, hobbies, business, computing and education.

British Library Cataloguing in Publication Data: a catalogue record for this title is available from the British Library.

Library of Congress Catalog Card Number: on file.

First published in UK 2004 by Hodder Arnold, 338 Euston Road, London, NW1 3BH.

First published in US 2005 by Contemporary Books, a division of the McGraw-Hill Companies, 1 Prudential Plaza, 130 East Randolph Street, Chicago, IL 60601 USA.

This edition published 2004.

The **teach yourself** name is a registered trade mark of Hodder Headline Ltd.

Author: Sue Tyson-Ward
Text and illustrations © Hodder & Stoughton Educational 2004

Printed and bound by Graphycems, Spain.

Impression number 10 9 8 7 6 5 4 3 2 1

Year 2010 2009 2008 2007 2006 2005 2004

CONTENTS

3

INTRODUCTION

This **Teach Yourself Portuguese Phrasebook** is an essential accessory for visitors to Portugal and other Portuguese-speaking countries, of whatever age and for whatever purpose. It provides a thorough survival guide with useful phrases in authentic but simple modern Portuguese, in clearly defined logical sections for quick and easy reference.

Features include:

- Up-to-date information sections about modern Portuguese life.

- A full alphabetical wordlist for quick reference.

- A simple, consistent and effective pronunciation guide.

- Key root sentences and phrases suitable for a variety of situations through substitution of appropriate vocabulary.

- Simple and effective questions to obtain short answers, avoiding confusion.

- Suggestions for some of the answers you might hear in response to your questions.

- A special general information reference section making this much more than just a phrasebook.

- A section of basic expressions suitable for many situations.

In Portuguese there is a difference between 'you' used formally (*o senhor/a senhora* (lit. the gentleman/the lady) and informally (*você*). Phrases and expressions employing one or the other are clearly indicated, and where both are suitable, both options are given.

Generally, Portuguese nouns end in **o** for masculine nouns and in **a** for feminine nouns. Where this is not the case, the wordlist section indicates clearly by the symbol **m** or **f** after the word in question.

Phrases which give masculine and feminine alternatives indicate the respective endings, such as:
obrigado/a; hence *obrigado* for men, and *obrigada* for women.
The pronunciation transcription also shows the differences:
oh-bree-gah-doo/uh

You can prepare yourself before your visit by practising a number of the more common basic expressions and becoming familiar with Portuguese pronunciation patterns outlined in the book, although it can be equally effective when used 'on site'.

Boa viagem!

PRONUNCIATION GUIDE

The sound of Portuguese has often been likened to Russian, or other East European languages such as Slovakian. It has a sing-song intonation and lots of nasal and shushing sounds, and is very different to listen to from its nearest neighbour, Spanish, despite the similarity in spelling of many of the words. Indeed, it has often been said that although the Portuguese can understand spoken Spanish, the Spanish have much more difficulty in deciphering spoken Portuguese. However, despite some of its intricacies, it is a fairly phonetic language; that means that once you get to grips with the different sounds of the letters, what you see is generally what you say – unlike English or French, for example, which have some tricky spellings and silent letters.

To help you with the phrases in this book, we have devised a transcription guide for every word to show you how each should be pronounced. This is not an exact science, however, as the letters in the English transcription may themselves be pronounced differently, depending on which part of the English-speaking world you come from. It is merely one attempt to get you nearer to the Portuguese sound. Ultimately, you should aim to note down your own sound system when you hear a new word, whether it be in Portugal itself or on tapes you may be using. That way, your transcriptions will be tailor-made using your own method for interpreting sounds. Bear in mind, too, that Portuguese may sound different depending on where the speaker comes from – the Algarve, in particular, has a specific sound system.

In the meantime, here are some transcriptions for trickier sounds used in this guide:

Symbol	Portuguese		English	Transcription	Example
a	*as in* casa	*compare with*	sister	uh	ka-<u>suh</u>
i	ir		week	ee	<u>eer</u>
ai	mais		(m)y	y	mysh
oi	oito		joint	oy	<u>oy</u>-too
ei	meia		May	ay	may-uh
au	bacalhau		sound	owu	ba-kal-<u>yowu</u>
ç	serviços		sun	s	ser-vee-<u>soosh</u>
nh	vinho		onion	n-y	vin-<u>yoo</u>
lh	mulher		million	l-y	mul-<u>yair</u>
ch	chocolate		shout	sh	<u>sho</u>-ko-lat
j	junho		pleasure	zh	zhoon-yoo
g	geléia		zh in Zhivago	zh	zheh-lay-uh

Nasal sounds

There are a number of sounds in Portuguese that are sounded in the nasal passage (as if you were holding your nose). These are denoted by an η.

Symbol		Portuguese	Transcription	Example
m	*as in*	tem com	mη or (mη)	taymη comη
ão		pão	owη [as in pound]	powη
õe		põe	oyη [as in point]	poyη
ui		muito	weeη	mweeηtoo
ã		lã	aη	laη

Other sounds

The letter 'h' is always silent in Portuguese.

An 's' at the end of a word or after a vowel usually makes a sh sound, unless by running it on to the following word it may lose some of the impact.

The transcriptions ah/eh/oh denote a softer, slightly more closed sound, said with the mouth less open than for a/e/o.

The letters 'ss' indicate the sound is more 'hissed' than a soft 's'.

The letters 'que' are pronounced either as kuh or, when running into a word with a vowel, kee.

Words beginning with 'es' sound more like sh; you rarely hear the 'e'.

The letters 'rr' and 'r' at the beginning of a word are either rolled, or pronounced with a guttural 'h' rather like the 'ch' in 'loch', depending on regional variation.

Transcriptions

In the transcriptions appearing in the following pages, hyphens separate two or more syllables in a word and stressed syllables are shown by underlines. Start by saying each syllable slowly, building up to a normal speaking speed.

USEFUL EVERYDAY PHRASES

THE BASICS

Yes/No	Sim/Não *seemη/nowη*
Please	Se faz favor/Por favor *suh fash fa-<u>vor</u>/por fa-<u>vor</u>*
Thank you	Obrigado/a *oh-bree-gah-doo/uh*
Thanks	Obrigadinho/a *oh-bree-gah-<u>deen</u>-yoo/uh*
Good morning	Bom dia *bomη <u>dee</u>-yuh*
Good afternoon	Boa tarde *<u>boh</u>-uh tard*
Good evening	Boa tarde/boa noite *<u>boh</u>-uh tard/<u>boh</u>-uh <u>noyt</u>*
Sorry	Perdão *per-<u>down</u>*
OK	Tudo bem/bem *<u>too</u>-doo baymη/baymη*

ASKING

Can you...?	Pode...? *pod...?*
Can I...?/May I...?	Posso...? *<u>poh</u>-ssoo...?*

Could you...?	Podia...?/Poderia...? *po-dee-yuh/po-duh-ree-yuh*

PROBLEMS, ASKING FOR HELP

I don't know	Não sei *nowη say*
Do you speak English?	Fala inglês? *fah-luh in-glaysh?*
I don't speak much Portuguese	Não falo muito português *nowη fah-loo mweeη-too port-too-gaysh*
I don't understand	Não compreendo *nowη com-pree-en-doo*
Do you understand?	Compreende? *com-pree-end?*
Can you help me?	Pode ajudar-me? *pod a-zhoo-dar-muh?*
Thanks for your help	Obrigado pela ajuda *oh-bree-gah-doo pay-luh uh-zhoo-duh*
Do you know...?	Sabe...? *sab...?*
Excuse me (get past someone)	Com licença *comη lee-sen-suh*
Excuse me (get attention)	Desculpe *desh-koolp*
I can't...	Não posso... *nowη poh-ssoo...*
Just a moment	Um momento *umη mo-men-too*

Speak more slowly, please	Fale mais devagar se faz favor *fal mysh duh-vuh-<u>gar</u> suh fash fa-<u>vor</u>*
Could you speak more loudly?	Pode falar mais alto? *pod fa-<u>lar</u> mysh <u>al</u>-too?*
Could you repeat that?	Pode repetir? *pod ruh-puh-<u>teer</u>?*
Pardon?	Como? *<u>com</u>-oo?*
I think so	Acho que sim *<u>ash</u>-oo kuh seemη*
Could you write that down?	Podia escrevê-lo? *po-<u>dee</u>-yuh sheve-<u>vay</u>-loo?*

GREETINGS AND MAKING FRIENDS

The Portuguese are quite formal when meeting and greeting people – it is customary to shake hands and use polite greetings. Friends and family kiss each other when they meet or say goodbye to each other. You may notice that the Portuguese are often more direct in their speech, especially in bars and shops, which can sometimes sound offhand.

People like to greet each other in passing whilst in the street – even with strangers. Try it yourself – a friendly 'Good morning' works wonders!

Good morning	Bom dia *bomη <u>dee</u>-yuh*
Good afternoon/evening	Boa tarde *<u>boh</u>-uh tard*
Good night	Boa noite *<u>boh</u>-uh noyt*
Hello/Hi	Olá! *oh-<u>la</u>!*
How are you? (formal)	Como está? *<u>com</u>-oo shta?*

How are you? (informal)	Tudo bem? _too_-doo baymη?
How are things?	Tudo bem? _too_-doo baymη?
Are you well?	Está bem? shta baymη?
I'm well, thanks	Estou bem, obrigado/a shtoh baymη, oh-bree-_gah_-doo/uh
Very well, thanks	Muito bem, obrigado/a _mween_-too baymη, oh-bree-_gah_-doo/uh
All right	Bem baymη
Not bad	Mais ou menos mysh oh _may_-noosh
I'm so-so	Mais ou menos mysh oh _may_-noosh
And you? (formal)	E o senhor/a senhora? ee oo sehn-_your_/uh sehn-_your_-uh?
And you? (informal)	E você?/E tu? ee voh-_say_?/ee too?
Is this seat occupied?	(Este lugar) Está ocupado? (esht loo-_gar_) shta oh-koo-_pa_-doo?
I am/My name is...	Chamo-me... _sha_-moo-muh...
What's your name?	Como se chama? _com_-oo suh _sha_-muh?
Pleased to meet you	Muito prazer _mween_-too pra-_zair_
One moment, please	Um momento, por favor oomη mo-_men_-too, por fa-_vor_

It doesn't matter	Não importa *nowη im-por-tuh*
I don't understand	Não compreendo *nowη comη-pree-en-doo*
Could you...?	Podia...? *po-dee-yuh...?*
...repeat that	...repetir *ruh-puh-teer*
...speak more slowly	...falar mais devagar *fa-lar mysh duh-vuh-gar*
...translate it into English	...traduzir para inglês *tra-doo-zeer puh-ruh in-glaysh*
I don't speak Portuguese	Não falo português *nowη fa-loo por-too-gaysh*
I speak a little Portuguese	Falo um pouco de português *fa-loo oomη poh-koo duh por-too-gaysh*
Do you speak English?	Fala inglês? *fa-luh in-glaysh?*
What is this called in Portuguese?	Como se chama isto em português? *com-oo suh sha-muh eesh-too aymη por-too-gaysh?*
Mr/Sir	(o) Senhor *(oo) sehn-your*
Mrs/Madam	(a) Senhora *(uh) sehn-your-uh*
Miss	(a) Senhora *(uh) sehn-your-uh*
This is...	Este é... *esht eh...*
...my husband	...o meu marido *oo may-oo mah-ree-doo*

...my fiancé	...o meu noivo *oo may-oo noy-voo*
...my boyfriend	...o meu namorado *oo may-oo na-moh-ra-doo*
...my partner	...o meu parceiro *oo may-oo par-say-roo*
...my (male) friend	...o meu amigo *oo may-oo a-mee-goo*
...my son	...o meu filho *oo may-oo feel-yoo*
This is...	Esta é... *eh-shtuh eh...*
...my wife	...a minha mulher *uh meen-yuh mul-yair*
...my fiancée	...a minha noiva *uh meen-yuh noy-vuh*
...my girlfriend	...a minha namorada *uh meen-yuh na-moh-ra-duh*
...my partner	...a minha parceira *uh meen-yuh par-say-ruh*
...my (female) friend	...a minha amiga *uh meen-yuh a-mee-guh*
...my daughter	...a minha filha *uh meen-yuh feel-yuh*
I'm...	Sou... *soh...*
...English	...inglês/inglesa *in-glaysh/in-glay-suh*
...Scottish	...escocês/escocesa *shco-saysh/shco-say-suh*
...Irish	...irlandês/irlandesa *eer-lan-daysh/eer-lan-day-suh*

...Welsh	...galês/galesa *ga-<u>laysh</u>/ga-<u>lay</u>-suh*
...American	...americano/a *a-meh-ree-<u>ka</u>-noo/uh*
...Canadian	...canadense *ka-na-<u>denss</u>*
...Australian	...australiano/a *owsh-tra-lee-<u>a</u>-noo/uh*
Are you (Portuguese)? (formal)	O senhor/ A senhora é português/portuguesa? *oo sehn-<u>your</u>/uh sehn-<u>your</u>-uh eh por-too-<u>gaysh</u>/por-too-<u>gay</u>-suh?*
Are you (Brazilian)? (informal)	Você é brasileiro/a? *voh-<u>say</u> eh brah-zee-<u>lay</u>-roo/uh?*
Where do you come from?	De onde é? *duh ond eh?*
I live...	Moro... *<u>moh</u>-roo...*
...in London	...em Londres *aymη <u>lon</u>-dresh*
...in New York	...na Nova Iorque *nuh <u>noh</u>-vuh york*
...in the north of England	...no norte da Inglaterra *noo nort duh in-gla-<u>tair</u>-ruh*
I have...	Tenho... *<u>tayn</u>-yoo...*
...a son/daughter	...um filho/uma filha *oomη <u>feel</u>-yoo/<u>oo</u>-muh feel-yuh*
...three children	...três filhos *traysh <u>feel</u>-yoosh*
I don't have any children	Não tenho filhos *nowη <u>tayn</u>-yoo <u>fil</u>-yoosh*

I'm single/married/divorced	Sou solteiro/a, casado/a, divorciado/a *soh sol-<u>tay</u>-roo/uh, cah-<u>sah</u>-doo/uh, dee-vor-see-<u>yah</u>-doo/uh*
I'm on holiday	Estou de férias *shtoh duh <u>feh</u>-ree-uhsh*
I work/live here	Trabalho/moro aqui *tra-<u>bal</u>-yoo/<u>moh</u>-roo a-<u>key</u>*
I'm a student	Sou estudante *soh shtu-<u>dant</u>*
I'm a businessman/woman	Sou homem/mulher de negócios *soh <u>oh</u>-memɲ/mul-<u>yair</u> duh neh- <u>goh</u>-see-yoosh*
I'm doing a course	Estou a frequentar um curso *shtoh uh freh-kwen-<u>tar</u> oomɲ <u>cur</u>-soo*
And you? (formal)	E o senhor/a senhora? *ee oo sehn-<u>your</u>/uh sehn-<u>your</u>-uh?*
And you? (informal)	E você? *ee voh-<u>say</u>?*
Would you like to...?	Quer...? *kair...?*
...dance	...dançar *dan-<u>ssar</u>*
...have something to eat/drink	...tomar alguma coisa *toh-<u>mar</u> al-<u>goo</u>-muh <u>coy</u>-suh*
...come out with me	...sair comigo *sy-<u>eer</u> coh-<u>mee</u>-goo*
...go out for dinner	...ir jantar *eer zhan-<u>tar</u>*
Do you fancy a drink?	Apetece-lhe beber alguma coisa? *a-peh-<u>tess</u>-lyuh buh-<u>bair</u> al-<u>goo</u>- muh <u>coy</u>-suh?*
I'm broke	Estou teso/a *shtoh <u>tay</u>-soo/uh*

I'll treat you	Pago eu *pah-goo ay-oo*
Where shall we meet?	Onde é que nos encontramos? *ond eh kuh noosh en-con-trah-moosh?*
Can I call you?	Posso chamá-lo/la? *poh-ssoo sha-ma-loo/luh?*
I'll pick you up	Vou buscá-lo/la *voh bush-ka-loo/luh?*
Sorted!	Combinado! *com-bee-nah-doo!*
No, thanks	Não, obrigado/a *nown, oh-bree-gah-doo/uh*
I can't	Não posso *nown poh-ssoo*
I haven't time	Não tenho tempo *nown tayn-yoo tem-poo*
I don't feel like it	Não me apetece *nown me a-peh-tess*
I've got something else on	Tenho outro compromisso *tayn-yoo oh-troo com-pro-mee-ssoo*
Goodbye	Adeus *a-day-oosh*
See you/Bye	Tchau *chow*
See you later	Até logo *uh-tay loh-goo*
See you tomorrow	Até amanhã *uh-tay uh-man-yan*
See you next time	Até à próxima *uh-tay a pro-ssee-muh*

I'm sick/tired of...	Estou farto/a de... *shtoh far-too/uh duh...*
This is a bit boring	Isto é um pouco chato *ish-too eh oomη poh-koo sha-too*
What a pain!	Que chatice/maçada! *kuh sha-teess/muh-ssa-duh!*
Brilliant!	Óptimo! *oh-tee-moo!*

For business language see page 173.

You may hear:

De nada *duh na-duh*	Don't mention it
Não faz mal *nowη fash mal*	That's all right
Gosta de cá estar? *gosh-tuh duh ka shtar?*	Do you like it here?

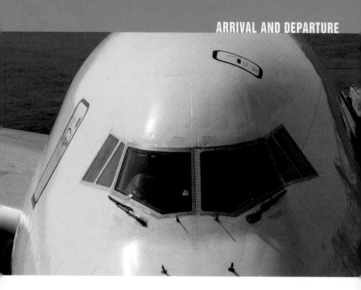

ARRIVAL AND DEPARTURE

Portugal is a member-state of the European Union and has the same customs regulations as any other EU country. EU citizens have free access into Portugal across borders but you still need your passport as your main form of identification, which you should carry with you at all times.

Anyone studying or working in Portugal requires written proof of their intentions.

Carry copies of important documents and photographs in at least triplicate.

Important signs at airports are also written in English.

Information about duty-free regulations are available at airports – they are the same as for other EU countries.

PASSPORT CONTROL

I'm/we're here...	Estou/Estamos cá... *shtoh/<u>shta</u>-moosh ka...*
...on holiday	...de férias *duh <u>feh</u>-ree-uhsh*
...on business	...em negócios *aymη neh-<u>goh</u>-see-yoosh*
...to visit friends	...para visitar amigos *<u>puh</u>-ruh vee-zee-<u>tar</u> a-<u>mee</u>-goosh*
I'm/We're going to stay...	Vou/Vamos ficar... *voh/<u>va</u>-moosh fee-<u>kar</u>...*
...for two weeks	...duas semanas *<u>doo</u>-uhsh suh-<u>mah</u>-nuhsh*
...for a month	...um mês *oomη may-sh*
This is my address	Esta é a minha morada *<u>eh</u>-shtuh eh uh <u>meen</u>-yuh mo-<u>ra</u>-duh*
I'm staying here...	Estou hospedado/a aqui *shtoh osh-pee-<u>dah</u>-doo/uh a-<u>key</u>*

LUGGAGE

Where are the trolleys?	Onde estão os carrinhos? *ond shtowη oosh ka-<u>rrin</u>-yoosh?*
I can't find...	Não posso encontrar... *nowη <u>poh</u>-ssoo en-con-<u>trar</u>...*
...my bag	...a minha mala de mão *uh <u>meen</u>-yuh <u>ma</u>-luh duh mowη*
...my suitcase	...a minha mala *uh <u>meen</u>-yuh <u>ma</u>-luh*
...my luggage	...a minha bagagem *uh <u>meen</u>-yuh buh-<u>ga</u>-zhaymη*

Could you help me with my luggage?	Podia ajudar-me com a bagagem? *po-<u>dee</u>-yuh a-zhoo-<u>dar</u>-muh com<u>η</u> uh buh-<u>ga</u>-zhaym<u>η</u>?*
It's this one	É esta *eh <u>eh</u>-shtuh*
How much do I owe you?	Quanto lhe devo? *<u>kwan</u>-too lyuh <u>day</u>-voo?*

AT THE INFORMATION DESK

Where is...?/Where are...?	Onde é...?/Onde são...? *ond eh.../ond sow<u>η</u>...?*
...the taxi rank	...a praça de táxis *uh <u>pra</u>-ssuh duh <u>tax</u>-eesh*
...the bus to the city centre	...o autocarro para o centro *oo ow-too-<u>karr</u>-oo <u>puh</u>-ruh oo <u>sen</u>-troo*
...the left luggage office	...o depósito de bagagens *oh duh-<u>poh</u>-see-too duh buh-<u>ga</u>-zhaynsh*
...the toilets	...os lavabos/sanitários *oosh la-<u>vah</u>-boosh/sa-nee-<u>ta</u>-ree-oosh*
Where can I/we...?	Onde posso/podemos...? *ond <u>poh</u>-ssoo/poh-<u>day</u>-moosh...?*
...buy a ticket	...comprar um bilhete *com-<u>prar</u> oom<u>η</u> bil-<u>yet</u>*
...change money	...trocar dinheiro *tro-<u>kar</u> deen-<u>yay</u>-roo*
...hire a car	...alugar um automóvel *a-loo-<u>gar</u> oom<u>η</u> ow-too-<u>moh</u>-vel*
...make a phone call	...fazer uma chamada *fa-<u>zair</u> <u>oo</u>-muh sha-<u>ma</u>-duh*
Could you give me...?	Podia dar-me...? *po-<u>dee</u>-yuh <u>dar</u>-muh...?*

Do you have...?	Tem...? *taymη...?*
...a bus timetable	...um horário de autocarros *oomη or-rah-ree-yoo duh ow-too-karr-oosh*
...a train timetable	...um horário de comboios *oomη or-rah-ree-yoo duh com-boy-oosh*
...a brochure of (of the town)	...um folheto de (da cidade) *oomη fol-yeh-too duh (duh see-da-duh)*
...a list of hotels	...uma lista de hotéis *oo-muh lish-tuh duh o-tay-yeesh*
Could you recommend a...hotel?	Podia recomendar um hotel...? *po-dee-yuh re-co-men-dar oomη o-tel...?*
...luxury	...de luxo *duh loo-shoo*
...three star	...de três estrelas *duh traysh shtre-lush*
...economic/cheap	...barato *ba-ra-too*
Can I book a hotel here?	Posso reservar um hotel aqui? *poh-ssoo re-sair-var oomη o-tel a-key?*

For more on hotels, see page 29.

ASKING THE WAY

Excuse me!	Desculpe! *desh-koolp!*
How do you get to...?	Como é que se vai para...? *com-oo eh kuh suh vye puh-ruh...?*

...Lagos

...Lagos
la-goosh

...the Hotel (Pedro)

...o Hotel (Pedro)
oo o-*tel* (*ped*-roo)

...the beach

...a praia
uh *pry*-yuh

...the airport

...o aeroporto
oo eh-ro-*por*-too

How many kilometres is it to Évora?

Évora fica a quantos quilómetros?
eh-vo-ruh *fee*-kuh uh *kwan*-toosh kee-*lo*-me-troosh?

Do you have a map/town plan?

Tem um mapa/um plano da cidade?
taymη oomη *ma*-puh/oomη *pla*-noo duh see-*da*-duh?

Where are the shops?

Onde ficam as lojas?
ond *fee*-camη uhsh *lo*-zhuhsh?

Is it a long way/nearby?

É longe/perto?
eh lonzh/*per*-too?

Do I have to take the bus/ underground?

Tenho de apanhar o autocarro/o metro?
tayn-yoo duh uh-pan-*yar* oo ow-too-*karr*-oo/oo *meh*-troo?

Can you walk there?

Pode-se ir a pé?
pod-suh eer uh pay?

Can you show me?

Pode mostrar-me?
pod mosh-*trar*-muh?

Where is...?

Onde fica...?
ond *fee*-kuh...?

...the railway station

...a estação de caminho de ferro
uh shta-*ssown*η duh ka-*meen*-yoo duh *fair*-roo

...the bus/coach station	...o terminal/a central de camionagem/estação de camionetas *oo tair-mee-<u>nal</u>/uh sen-<u>tral</u> duh ka-mee-oh-<u>nah</u>-zhaymη/shta-<u>ssow</u>η duh ka-mee-oh-<u>neh</u>-tuhsh*
...the underground	...o metro *oo <u>meh</u>-troo*
...the motorway to Lisbon	...a autoestrada para Lisboa *uh ow-too-esh-<u>tra</u>-duh <u>puh</u>-ruh lizh-<u>bo</u>-uh*
...the main road/dual carriageway to Lagos	...a estrada para Lagos *uh <u>shtra</u>-duh <u>puh</u>-ruh <u>la</u>-goosh*
...the Beja road/way to Beja	...o caminho para Beja *oo ka-<u>meen</u>-yoo <u>puh</u>-ruh <u>bay</u>-zhuh*
...the tourist office	...o posto de turismo *oo posh-too duh too-<u>rizh</u>-moo*
...the town centre	...o centro da cidade *oo <u>sen</u>-troo duh see-<u>da</u>-duh*
...the police station	...a esquadra da polícia *uh <u>shkwa</u>-druh duh pol-<u>ee</u>-syuh*
Is there a/Are there...here (near here)?	Há...(por aqui)? *ah...(por a-<u>key</u>)?*
Where is there...?	Onde há...? *ond ah...?*
...a bank	...um banco *oomη <u>ban</u>-koo*
...a post office	...um correios *oomη ko-<u>ray</u>-yoosh*
...a car park	...um parque de estacionamento *oomη park duh shta-see-oh-nuh-<u>men</u>-too*

...a supermarket	...um supermercado *oomŋ soo-per-mur-<u>ka</u>-doo*
...a telephone booth	...uma cabine telefónica (um telefone) *<u>oo</u>-muh ka-<u>been</u> tel-ee-<u>fon</u>-ee-kuh (oomŋ te-le-<u>fon</u>)*

For more on shops see page 127.

You may hear:

Tome *tom*	Take
Vire/Volte/Corte *veer-volt-cort*	Turn
Siga em frente *<u>see</u>-guh aymŋ frent*	Carry straight on
Atravesse *a-tra-<u>vess</u>*	Cross
Passe *pass*	Pass
Continue *con-tin-<u>oo</u>-uh*	Continue
A primeira (rua) *uh pree-<u>may</u>-ruh (<u>roo</u>-uh)*	The first (street/road)
A segunda *uh se-<u>gun</u>-duh*	The second
A terceira *uh tair-<u>say</u>-ruh*	The third
À esquerda *a <u>shkair</u>-duh*	On the left
À direita *a dee-<u>ray</u>-tuh*	On the right
Em frente *aymŋ frent*	Straight on

| Ali
a-lee | There |
| (mesmo) Aqui
(*mezh*-moo) a-*key* | (just) Here |
| Aos semáforos
owsh se-ma-fuh-roosh | At the traffic lights |
| Ao fim da rua
ow feemη duh roo-uh | At the end of the street |
| À esquina
a shkee-nuh | On/At the corner |
| A (20) quilómetros
uh (vint) kee-lo-me-troosh | (20) kilometres away |
| A (10) minutos
uh (desh) mee-noo-toosh | (10) minutes away |
| Não é longe
nowη eh lonzh | It's not far |
| É perto (de)…
eh per-too (duh)… | It's near (to)… |
| A pé/De autocarro/De táxi
uh pay/duh ow-too-karr-oo/duh tax-ee | On foot/By bus/By taxi |
| Seria melhor apanhar um táxi
se-ree-yuh mel-yor uh-pan-yar umη tax-ee | It would be better to catch a taxi |

You may see:

Aberto	Open
Avariado	Broken (down)
Cuidado	Be careful
Entrada	Entrance
Empurre	Push
Fechado/Encerrado	Closed

Homens/Senhoras	Men's/Women's toilets
Informações	Information
Lavabos/Sanitários/WC	Toilets
Livre	Free
Não pise a relva	Keep off the grass
Ocupado	Engaged
Peões	Pedestrians
Perigo	Danger
Privado	Private
Proibido fumar	No smoking
Puxe	Pull
Reservado	Reserved
Saída (de emergência)	(emergency) Exit
S.F.F. (Se faz favor)	Please

ACCOMMODATION

HOTELS AND YOUTH HOSTELS

There are many different kinds of accommodation in Portugal, each offering a range of services and levels of comfort:

Hotel (H)	Hotel, ranked with 1–5 stars
(Hotel) Residencial/Residência (HR)	Guest house
Pensão (P)	Cheaper guest house, although they can be up to 4 star

At any of the above, you may sometimes find breakfast is served, but you need to check whether the price of the room includes any meals. Not all rooms will have en-suite facilities.

Pousada	State-run system of luxury hotels, most based in former historical buildings such as monasteries, or in areas of outstanding natural beauty
Albergaria/Estalagem	Inn
Pousada de Juventude	Youth hostel
Turismo de Habitação	A network in northern Portugal, where you can stay in family country homes, often stately homes and manor houses
Turismo Rural	Again in the north, where you can stay with families in the countryside
Agroturismo	Working farms
Quartos	Rooms rented out in homes

Local tourist offices usually have lists of available accommodation, and will often help you to book a room. A number of independent websites now also provide booking details.

The daily room rate should be displayed on a notice on the back of the door, although breakfast is not always included. Where it is, it will be continental, with a selection of bread rolls and jams, cakes, sometimes ham and cheese, fruit and drinks.

Many hotels still request that you leave your passport with them, once you have filled in a booking form at reception. As your only official form of ID in Portugal, it is better to carry it with you if you can, but if not, keep a supply of photocopies available in case of problems.

Not all hotels, especially smaller family-run ones in rural areas, accept payment by credit card; check first, so that you can make arrangements to get hold of cash before checking out.

You will need an adaptor to use electrical appliances such as hairdryers. The voltage in Portugal is 220V.

BOOKING A ROOM

Have you any rooms free?	Tem quartos vagos? *taymη kwar-toosh vah-goosh?*
I/We have a reservation	Tenho/Temos um quarto reservado *tayn-yoo/tay-moosh oomη kwar-too re-sair-va-doo*
I/We would like to make a reservation	Queria/Queríamos reservar um quarto *kree-uh/kree-uh-moosh re-sair-var oomη kwar-too*
My name is...	O meu nome é... *oo may-oo nom eh...*
Is there another hotel nearby?	Há outro hotel por aqui? *ah oh-troo o-tel por a-key?*
I/We would like a single/double room	Queria/Queríamos um quarto individual/de casal *kree-uh/kree-uh-moosh oomη kwar-too in-dee-vee-doo-al/duh kah-sal*
We would like two rooms	Queríamos dois quartos *kree-uh-moosh doysh kwar-toosh*
I/We would like a room...	Queria/Queríamos um quarto... *kree-uh/kree-uh-moosh oomη kwar-too...*
...with a double bed	...com cama de casal *comη kah-muh duh kah-sal*
...with two beds	...com duas camas *comη doo-uhsh kah-muhsh*
...for three people	...para três pessoas *puh-ruh traysh pe-ssoh-uhsh*
...with a cot	...com cama de criança *comη kah-muh duh cree-yan-ssuh*

...with a bath	...com banheira *com̨ ban-<u>yay</u>-ruh*
...with a shower	...com duche *com̨ doosh*
...at the back/front	...aos fundos/à frente *owsh <u>fun</u>-doosh/a frent*
...with a sea view	...com vista para o mar *com̨ <u>vish</u>-tuh <u>puh</u>-ruh oo mar*
...with a balcony	...com varanda *com̨ vuh-<u>ran</u>-duh*
(It's) for...	(É) para... *(eh) <u>puh</u>-ruh...*
...one night	...uma noite *<u>oo</u>-muh noyt*
...two nights	...duas noites *<u>doo</u>-uhsh <u>noy</u>-tuhsh*
...one week	...uma semana *<u>oo</u>-muh suh-<u>mah</u>-nuh*
...a fortnight	...quinze dias *kinz <u>dee</u>-yuhsh*
How much is it?	Quanto é? *<u>kwan</u>-too eh?*
per person/per night?	por pessoa/por noite? *por peh-<u>ssoh</u>-uh/por noyt?*
Can you write it down?	Pode escrevê-lo? *pod shcre-<u>vay</u>-loo?*
Is there a supplementary charge for another bed?	Há suplemento para uma cama extra? *ah su-plee-<u>men</u>-too <u>puh</u>-ruh oo- muh <u>kah</u>-muh <u>esh</u>-truh?*
Is there a charge for the child?	A criança tem que pagar? *uh cree-<u>yan</u>-ssuh taym̨ kuh puh-<u>gar</u>?*

He/She is...	Ele/Ela tem...
	el/el-uh taymη...
...six months old	...seis meses
	saysh may-zesh
...one year old	...um ano
	oomη a-noo
...seven years old	...sete anos
	set a-noosh
Do you accept credit cards?	Aceitam cartões de crédito?
	a-say-tamη kar-toyηsh duh cre-dee-too?
Can I/we see the room?	Posso/Podemos ver o quarto?
	poh-ssoo/poh-day-moosh vair oo kwar-too?
I/We will (won't) take it	(não) Fico/Ficamos com o quarto
	(nowη) fee-koo/fee-ka-moosh comη oo kwar-too
It's...	É...
	eh...
...rather/very expensive	...um pouco/muito caro
	oomη poh-koo/mwee-too kah-roo
...too small	...demasiado pequeno
	deh-mah-see-ah-doo pe-kay-noo
...dark	...escuro
	shcoo-roo
...noisy	...barulhento
	bah-rul-yen-too
...stuffy	...abafado
	ah-buh-fah-doo
Do you have another room?	Tem outro quarto?
	taymη oh-troo kwar-too?

Could you take the luggage to the room, please?	Pode levar a bagagem ao quarto, por favor? *pod le-<u>var</u> uh buh-<u>ga</u>-zhaymη ow <u>kwar</u>-too, por fa-<u>vor</u>?*
Is breakfast included?	O pequeno almoço está incluído? *oo pe-<u>kay</u>-noo al-<u>moh</u>-ssoo shta in-kloo-<u>ee</u>-doo?*
I/We'd like...	Queria/Queríamos... *<u>kree</u>-uh/<u>kree</u>-uh-moosh...*
...breakfast only	...só dormida com pequeno almoço *soh dor-<u>mee</u>-duh comη pe-<u>kay</u>-noo al-<u>moh</u>-ssoo*
...half board	...meia pensão *<u>may</u>-uh pen-<u>sown</u>*
...full board	...pensão completa *pen-<u>sown</u> com-<u>play</u>-tuh*
Is there...?	Há...? *ah...?*
...air conditioning	...ar condicionado *ar con-dee-see-yoh-<u>na</u>-doo*
...a lift	...elevador *uh-lev-vuh-<u>dor</u>*
...a safe	...um cofre *oomη <u>cof</u>-ray*

ROOM SERVICE AND MEALS

What time is...?	A que horas servem...? *uh kay <u>or</u>-ush <u>sair</u>-vaymη...?*
...breakfast	...o pequeno almoço *oo pe-<u>kay</u>-noo al-<u>moh</u>-ssoo*
...lunch	...o almoço *oo al-<u>moh</u>-ssoo*

…dinner	…o jantar *oo zhan-<u>tar</u>*
Could you bring breakfast to the room?	Podia trazer o pequeno almoço ao quarto? *po-<u>dee</u>-yuh tra-<u>zair</u> oo pe-<u>kay</u>-noo al-<u>moh</u>-ssoo ow <u>kwar</u>-too?*
Could you call me/us…?	Podia chamar-me/chamar-nos…? *po-<u>dee</u>-yuh sha-<u>mar</u>-muh/sha-<u>mar</u>-noosh…?*
…for breakfast	…para o pequeno almoço *<u>puh</u>-ruh oo pe-<u>kay</u>-noo al-<u>moh</u>-ssoo*
…at half past seven	…às sete e meia *azh set ee <u>may</u>-uh*
Can I have the key (for number ten) please?	A chave (do quarto dez) por favor? *uh shav (doo <u>kwar</u>-too desh) por fa-<u>vor</u>?*
Do you have/Could you get…?	Tem/Podia arranjar…? *taymη/po-<u>dee</u>-yuh a-ran-<u>zhar</u>…?*
…an ashtray	…um cinzeiro *oomη sin-<u>zay</u>-roo*
…another blanket	…outro cobertor *<u>oh</u>-troo coh-ber-<u>tor</u>*
…a clothes hanger	…um cabide *oomη ca-<u>beed</u>*
…another pillow	…mais uma almofada *mysh <u>oo</u>-muh al-moh-<u>fah</u>-duh*
…some soap	…sabão *sa-<u>bowη</u>*
…another towel	…mais uma toalha *mysh <u>oo</u>-muh toh-<u>al</u>-yuh*

...a hairdryer	...um secador de cabelos *oomη se-kah-<u>dor</u> duh kuh-<u>beh</u>-loosh*
...an iron	...um ferro *oomη <u>fair</u>-roo*
Could you...?	Podia...? *po-<u>dee</u>-yuh...?*
...put this in the safe	...guardar isto no cofre *gwar-<u>dar</u> <u>eesh</u>-too noo <u>cof</u>-ray*
...call a taxi	...chamar um táxi *sha-<u>mar</u> oomη <u>tax</u>-ee*
...bring the luggage	...trazer a bagagem *tra-<u>zair</u> uh buh-<u>ga</u>-zhaymη*
...get the bill ready (for tomorrow)	...preparar a conta (para amanhã) *pre-puh-<u>rar</u> uh <u>con</u>-tuh (<u>puh</u>-ruh uh-man-<u>yaη</u>)*
Are there any messages for me?	Há recados para mim? *ah re-<u>kah</u>-doosh <u>puh</u>-ruh meemη?*

QUERIES AND COMPLAINTS

The toilet paper has run out	Acabou-se o papel higiénico *a-ka-<u>boh</u>-suh oo puh-<u>pel</u> ee-zhee-<u>yen</u>-ee-koo*
There aren't any (bath towels)	Não há (toalhas de banho) *nowη ah (toh-<u>al</u>-yuhsh duh <u>ban</u>-yoo)*
There's (a pillow) missing	Falta (uma almofada) *<u>fal</u>-tuh (<u>oo</u>-muh al-moh-<u>fah</u>-duh)*
The light/lamp doesn't work	O candeeiro não funciona *oo can-dee-<u>yay</u>-roo nowη fun-ssee-<u>oh</u>-nuh*
The tap is dripping	A torneira está a pingar *uh tor-<u>nay</u>-ruh shta uh pin-<u>gar</u>*

CHECKING OUT

Can I have the bill, please?	Posso ter a conta, por favor? *poh-ssoo tair uh con-tuh, por fa-vor?*
Room number...	O quarto número... *oo kwar-too noo-muh-roo...*
I think that the bill is wrong	Creio que a conta está errada *cray-oo kuh uh con-tuh shta eh-rah-duh*
Excuse me, but there's a mistake	Desculpe, mas há um erro *desh-koolp, msh ah oomη eh-roo*
Could I have an invoice?	Posso ter uma factura? *poh-ssoo tair oo-muh fak-too-ruh?*

CAMPING AND CARAVANNING

Campsites are very busy during the summer months, so it is advisable to book in advance.

The useful guide Roteiro Campista, on sale in most bookshops, details all the sites in Portugal, together with contact addresses and phone numbers. You can also get advice from the Portuguese Tourist Office in Portugal, or at ICEP, Portuguese Trade & Tourism Office, 22–25a Sackville Street, London W1X 2LY. Tel: 020-7494-5720.

Many sites close in the winter, so you will need to check the length of the season of where you intend to stay.

Sites have different tariffs, most with English versions, so you have a clear indication of what charges apply for certain combinations of vehicles/people/facilities. Younger children usually have a discount. Holders of UK Caravan Club membership have access to a wider choice of sites, as some only admit permit-holders. Apply for membership via The Camping and Caravanning Club of Great Britain. In the Algarve, camping is only permitted at recognised campsites. Elsewhere, it is possible to camp outside official sites provided you show respect for the location.

I/We have a reservation	Reservei/Reservámos um lugar *re-sair-vay/re-sair-vah-moosh oomη loo-gar*
Can I/we see the campsite?	Posso/Podemos ver o parque? *poh-ssoo/poh-day-moosh vair oo park?*
Have you spaces free?	Tem lugares vagos? *taymη loo-gar-esh vah-goosh?*
Could you give me a leaflet with the prices?	Podia dar-me um folheto com a tarifa? *po-dee-yuh dar-muh oomη fol-yeh-too comη uh tuh-ree-fuh?*
I/We have...	Tenho/Temos... *tayn-yoo/tay-moosh...*
...a small/large tent	...uma tenda pequena/grande *oo-muh ten-duh puh-kay-nuh/grand*
...a caravan	...uma caravana *oo-muh kah-ruh-vah-nuh*
...a car	...um carro *oomη kah-roo*
...a campervan	...um carro-cama *oomη kah-roo-kah-muh*
How much is it...?	Quanto é...? *kwan-too eh...?*
...per person	...por pessoa *por peh-ssoh-uh*
...per day	...por dia *por dee-yuh*
...for a child	...para uma criança *puh-ruh oo-muh cree-yan-ssuh*
...for the tent	...para a tenda *puh-ruh uh ten-duh*

...for the car	...para o carro
	puh-ruh oo _kah_-roo
It's for...	É para...
	eh _puh_-ruh...
...two adults	...dois adultos
	doysh a-_dul_-toosh
...and a child	...e uma criança
	ee _oo_-muh cree-_yan_-ssuh
...three nights	...três noites
	traysh _noy_-tush
I/We prefer to be...	Prefiro/Prefirimos estar...
	pruh-_fee_-roo/pruh-feh-_ree_-moosh
	shtar...
...in the shade	...à sombra
	a _som_-bruh
...near the beach	...perto da praia
	per-too duh _pry_-uh
...away from the road	...longe da estrada
	lonzh duh _shtra_-duh
Do you have/rent...?	Tem/Aluga...?
	taymη/a-_loo_-guh...?
...tents	...tendas
	ten-duhsh
...caravans	...caravanas
	kah-ruh-_vah_-nuhsh
...a safe	...um cofre
	oomη _coh_-fray
...groundsheets	...oleados
	oh-lee-_ya_-doosh
...a torch	...uma lanterna de bolso
	_oo_-muh lan-_tair_-nuh duh _bol_-ssoo

...airbeds	...camas infláveis _ka_-muhsh in-_fla_-vay-eesh
...bottles of gas	...garrafas de gás guh-_ra_-fuhsh duh gash
...mosquito nets	...mosquiteiros mosh-kee-_tay_-roosh
Does the campsite close at night?	O parque fecha à noite? oo park _fay_-shuh a _noyt_?
At what time?	A que horas? uh kay _or_-uhsh?
Is/Are there...?	Há...? ah...?
...medical assistance	...assistência médica a-siss-_ten_-see-yuh _meh_-dee-kuh
...a first aid box	...uma caixa de primeiros-socorros _oo_-muh _kye_-shuh duh pree-_may_-roosh-soh-_koh_-roosh
...ice	...gelo _zhe_-loo
...a bar	...um bar oomη bar
...a children's play area	...um jardim infantil oomη zhah-_dimη_ in-fan-_teel_
Where is/are...?	Onde é/são...? ond eh/sowη...?
...the laundry	...a lavandaria uh luh-van-duh-_ree_-yuh
...the showers	...os duches oosh _doosh_-esh
...the kitchen facilities	...o lugar para cozinhar oo loo-_gar_ _puh_-ruh koh-zin-_yar_
...the rubbish bins	...os caixotes de lixo oosh kye-_shoh_-tush duh _lee_-shoo

...the toilets

...os lavabos/os sanitários
  oosh la-vah-boosh/oosh sa-nee-ta-ree-oosh

You may hear:

O parque está esgotado
oo park shta shgoh-tah-doo

The site is full

Não há vagas
nown ah vah-guhsh

There are no places

Para quantas noites?
puh-ruh kwan-tuhsh noy-tush?

For how many nights?

Quanto tempo vão ficar?
kwan-too tem-poo vown fee-kar?

How long are you staying?

Para quantas pessoas?
puh-ruh kwan-tuhsh pe-ssoh-uhsh?

For how many people?

Tudo está incluído
too-doo shta in-kloo-ee-doo

Everything is included

Faça favor de assinar aqui
fa-ssuh fa-vor duh a-ssin-ar a-key

Sign here, please

Podia preencher esta ficha?
po-dee-yuh pray-en-shair eh-shtuh fee-shuh?

Could you fill in this form?

Tem carnet/carta?
taymη kar-nay/car-tuh?

Do you have a membership card?

O seu passaporte, por favor
oo say-oo pass-uh-port, por fa-vor

Your passport, please

Pode escolher o lugar
pod shcol-yair oo loo-gar

You can pick your site

You may see:

Água corrente

Running water

Água potável

Drinking water

Caravanas	Caravans
Categoria 1/2/3	1st, 2nd, 3rd class
De luxo	Luxury
É proibido acampar	No camping allowed
Esgotado/lotado	No spaces/full
Lavabos	Washrooms
Lavandaria	Laundry
Livro de reclamações	Complaints book
Parque de campismo	Campsite
Recepção	Reception
Tarifa	Charges
Vagas	Spaces

VILLAS AND APARTMENTS

Self-catering accommodation is usually one of the following:

Aldeamento Turístico	Self-contained complex with its own facilities and classed L (luxury) and 1st and 2nd class
Apartamentos Turísticos	Self-catering flats in modern buildings
Apart-hotel	Self-catering flats inside hotels with cleaning services
Privately-owned and advertised accommodation for holiday lets, or longer term.	These are advertised in papers, or on the buildings themselves. Some are run by holiday companies, especially the villas and more luxurious homes.
I/We would like an apartment…	Queria/Queríamos um apartamento… _kree_-uh/_kree_-uh-moosh oomη a-par-ta-_men_-too…

...with 1/2/3 bedroom/s	...com 1/2/3 quarto/s *comη oomη/doysh/traysh* *<u>kwar</u>-too/sh*
...for two people	...para duas pessoas *<u>puh</u>-ruh <u>doo</u>-uhsh pe-<u>ssoh</u>-uhsh*
...for a month	...para um mês *<u>puh</u>-ruh oomη maysh*
What floor is it on?	Em que piso/andar é? *aymη kuh <u>pee</u>-soo/an-<u>dar</u> eh?*
I/We prefer the first floor/the top floor	Prefiro/Preferimos o primeiro andar/o último andar *pruh-<u>fee</u>-roo/pruh-feh-<u>ree</u>-moosh oo pree-<u>may</u>-roo an-<u>dar</u>/oo <u>ul</u>-tee-moo an-<u>dar</u>*
How many beds are there?	Há quantas camas? *ah <u>kwan</u>-tuhsh <u>ka</u>-muhsh?*
How many bedrooms are there?	Há quantos quartos? *ah <u>kwan</u>-toosh <u>kwar</u>-toosh?*
Is...included?	(O/A)...está incluído/a? *(oo/uh)...shta in-kloo-<u>ee</u>-doo/uh?*
...everything	...tudo *<u>too</u>-doo*
...the gas	...o gás *oo gash*
...the water	...a água *uh <u>a</u>-gwa*
...the electricity	...a electricidade *uh ee-lek-tree-see-<u>dad</u>*
...the rubbish collection	...a recolha de lixo *uh reh-<u>kol</u>-yuh duh <u>lee</u>-shoo*
...the cleaning	...a limpeza *uh lim-<u>pay</u>-zuh*
When is it cleaned?	Quando fazem a limpeza? *<u>kwan</u>-doo <u>fa</u>-zaymη uh lim-<u>pay</u>-zuh?*

Does it have...?	Tem...?
	taymη...?
...a balcony	...varanda
	...vuh-<u>ran</u>-duh
...central heating	...aquecimento central
	...a-kay-see-<u>men</u>-too sen-<u>tral</u>
...air conditioning	...ar condicionado
	...ar con-dee-see-yoh-<u>na</u>-doo
...a bath	...banheira
	...ban-<u>yay</u>-ruh
Is it fully equipped?	Está bem equipado?
	shta baymη eh-key-<u>pah</u>-doo?
Does it have electricity/gas?	Tem electricidade/gás?
	taymη ee-lek-tree-see-<u>dad</u>/gash?
Is/Are there...?	Há...?
	ah...?
...bedclothes	...roupa de cama
	...<u>roh</u>-puh duh <u>kah</u>-muh
...crockery	...louça
	...<u>loh</u>-suh
...cutlery	...talheres
	...tal-<u>yair</u>-esh
...any furniture	...móveis
	...<u>moh</u>-vay-ish
...towels	...toalhas
	...toh-<u>al</u>-yuhsh
...a washing machine	...uma máquina de lavar roupa
	...<u>oo</u>-muh <u>ma</u>-kee-nuh duh luh-<u>var</u> <u>roh</u>-puh
...a dishwasher	...um lava-louça
	...oomη <u>lah</u>-vuh-<u>loh</u>-suh
...access to a swimming pool	...aceso a uma piscina
	...a-<u>sess</u>-oo uh <u>oo</u>-muh pee-<u>ssee</u>-nuh

How much is the rent?	Quanto é o aluguer?
	kwan-too eh oo a-loo-gair?
Is there a deposit?	Há depósito?
	ah duh-poh-see-too?
The bill, please	A conta, por favor
	uh con-tuh por fa-vor
I'm/we're going...	Vou/Vamos...
	voh/va-moosh...
...this afternoon/this evening	...esta tarde/esta noite
	...eh-shtuh tard/eh-shtuh noyt
...tomorrow	...amanhã
	...uh-mun-yan

PROBLEMS

There isn't any gas/(hot) water	Não há gás/água (quente)
	nown ah gash/a-gwa (kent)
The...is not working	O/A...não funciona
	oo/uh...nown fun-ssee-oh-nuh
The...is broken (down)	O/A...está estragado (avariado)
	oo/uh...shta shtra-gah-doo (a-vah-ree-ah-doo)
...cooker	...o fogão
	...oo foh-gown
...light (electricity)	...a luz
	...uh loozh
...telephone	...o telefone
	...oo te-le-fon
...basin	...o lavatório
	...oo lah-vuh-tor-ree-yoo
....sink	...a pia
	...uh pee-yuh
...tap	...a torneira
	...uh tor-nay-ruh

...bath

...a banheira
uh ban-yay-ruh

...toilet

...a sanita
uh sah-nee-tuh

...shower

...o chuveiro
oo shoo-vay-roo

Can you repair it?

Pode reparrá-lo?
pod reh-puh-rah-loo?

It's dirty/damp/dark/cold

Está sujo/úmido/escuro/frio
shta soo-zhoo/oo-mee-doo/shcoo-roo/free-oo

Do you have an alternative?

Tem outro (apartamento)?
taymη oh-troo (a-par-ta-men-too)?

How much do I/we owe you?

Quanto lhe devo/devemos?
kwan-too lyuh day-voo/deh-vay-moosh?

You may hear:

Não temos quartos/apartamentos
nowη tay-moosh kwar-toosh/a-par-ta-men-toosh

We don't have rooms/apartments

Para quanto tempo?
puh-ruh kwan-too tem-poo?

For how long?

Para quantas pessoas?
puh-ruh kwan-tuhsh pe-ssoh-uhsh?

For how many people?

Tudo está incluído
too-doo shta in-kloo-ee-doo

Everything is included

Faça favor de assinar aqui
fa-ssuh fa-vor duh a-ssin-ar a-key

Sign here, please

Podia preencher esta ficha?
po-dee-yuh pray-en-shair eh-shtuh fee-shuh?

Could you fill in this form?

O seu passaporte, por favor
oo say-yoo pass-uh-port, por fa-vor

Your passport, please

Não podemos repará-lo
*now*η *poh-day-moosh reh-puh-rah-loo*

We cannot repair it

Aqui estão as chaves
*a-key shtow*η *uhsh sha-vesh*

Here are the keys

Limpamos todos os dias/
duas vezes por semana
*lim-pah-moosh toh-doosh oosh
dee-yuhsh/doo-uhsh vay-zesh por
se-ma-nuh*

It is cleaned every day/twice
a week

You may see:

Aldeia turística	Holiday village
Aluga-se	For rent
Condomínio fechado	Private/enclosed complex
Não há vagas/esgotado	No vacancies
Mobilado	Furnished
Para férias	For holidays
Piso/Apartamento	Flat
Remodelado	Renovated
Rés-do-chão	Ground floor
Saída de emergência	Emergency exit
Totalmente equipado	Fully equipped
Vivenda	Villa

TRAVEL

ROAD

When driving in Portugal, you must have with you at all times
your passport (as ID), driving licence, insurance documents,
registration details of the car and, if you are driving someone
else's car, a letter giving you permission to use it.

Insurance is vital in Portugal, as accidents occur frequently. You
will need 'Green Card' cover, available from your insurer. Check
that you are also covered for breakdown, as these kinds of
services can be very expensive. Members of the AA or RAC,
however, can receive breakdown assistance from the equivalent
Portuguese association (ACP). You must be 23 years old and
have been driving for one year to drive a hire car in Portugal.
Traffic drives on the right. Seat belts are compulsory and you
must carry a red warning triangle, in case of accident or
breakdown.

Many Portuguese roads are improving and there are a number of toll motorways. The Via Verde lane at tolls is only for those people who have a special account to allow them to pass through with a card. Motorways (*autoestradas*) are indicated by 'A' + the number. Main roads (*estradas*) are coded 'EN', or upgraded ones are 'IP' or 'IC'. Direct international routes are indicated by 'E'.

The maximum speed limit for cars is 60kph in towns, 90kph in other areas and 120kph on motorways.

Motorways have SOS phones, with access to breakdown services.

City-centre congestion is a problem in many towns and parking can be very difficult. Look out for the blue 'P' signs for official car parks and on-street pay and display areas. Fines are readily dished out for people who park in restricted areas.

FILLING STATION/GARAGE

There are many large self-service petrol stations throughout Portugal, although they are scarcer in country areas – here you may just find the odd small business.

The national chain (GALP) and garages such as BP, which is widespread, offer a range of services at their larger stations and accept payment by credit card. Some have prepayment machines.

Petrol is sold as: leaded (*gasolina-super*), unleaded (*sem chumbo*), and diesel (*gasóleo*).

Where is there...?	Onde há...? *ond ah...?*
...a car park	...um parque de estacionamento *oomη park duh shta-see-oh-nuh-men-too*
...a garage	...uma oficina de reparos *oo-muh oh-fee-see-nuh duh reh-pah-roosh*
...a petrol station	...uma estação de serviço *oo-muh shta-ssowη duh sair-vee-ssoo*

...a petrol garage (smaller)	...uma bomba de gasolina ..._oo_-muh _bom_-buh duh gah-soh-_lee_-nuh
Fill her up!	Encha, por favor! _en_-shuh, por fa-_vor_!
(5) litres of...	(Cinco) litros de... (_sin_-koo) _lee_-troosh duh...
(20) Euros of...	(Vinte) euros de... vint _air_-roosh duh...
...4 star	...super ..._soo_-per
...2 star	...normal ...nor-_mal_
...unleaded	...sem chumbo ...saymη _shum_-boo
...diesel	...gasóleo ...gah-_zoh_-lee-yoo
A litre of oil, please	Um litro de óleo, por favor oomη _lee_-troo duh _oh_-lee-yoo, por fa-_vor_
How much is it?	Quanto é? _kwan_-too eh?
Do you take...?	Aceitam...? a-_say_-tamη...?
...credit cards	...cartões de crédito ...kar-_toyη_sh duh _cre_-dee-too
...cheques	...cheques ..._sheh_-kush
Could you check...?	Podia verificar...? po-_dee_-yuh veh-ree-fee-_kar_...?
...the water	...a água ...uh _a_-gwa

...the oil	...o óleo
	...oo <u>oh</u>-lee-yoo
...the battery	...a bateria
	...uh bah-tuh-<u>ree</u>-yuh
...the tyres	...os pneus
	...oosh puh-<u>nay</u>-yoosh
...the radiator	...o radiador
	...oo ra-dee-a-<u>dor</u>
...the windscreen wipers	...as limpa pára-brisas
	...uhsh <u>lim</u>-puh <u>pa</u>-ruh-<u>bree</u>-suhsh
Could you...?	Podia...?
	po-<u>dee</u>-yuh...?
...clean the windows	...limpar os vidros
	...lim-<u>par</u> oosh <u>vee</u>-droosh
...wash the car	...lavar o carro
	...lah-<u>var</u> oo <u>kah</u>-roo
Do you have...?	Tem...?
	taymη...?
...a car wash	...lavagem automática
	...lah-<u>vah</u>-zhaymη ow-too-<u>mah</u>-tee-kuh
...an air pump	...bomba de ar
	...<u>bom</u>-buh duh ar
...toilets	...sanitários
	...sa-nee-<u>ta</u>-ree-oosh
...a telephone	...telefone
	...te-le-<u>fon</u>
Do you sell...?	Vende...?
	vend...?
...maps	...mapas
	...<u>ma</u>-puhsh

...cigarettes	...cigarros *...see-gah-roosh*
...drinks	...bebidas *...beh-bee-duhsh*

BREAKDOWN

Look for the signs *Oficina de reparos* and *Garagem*.

Where's the nearest garage?	Onde fica a oficina mais próxima? *ond fee-kuh uh oh-fee-see-nuh* *mysh pro-ssee-muh?*
I've had...	Tive... *teev...*
...an accident	...um acidente *...oomη a-see-dent*
...a breakdown	...uma avaria *...oo-muh a-vuh-ree-yuh*
...a puncture	...um furo *...oomη fu-roo*
I don't have a spare wheel	Não tenho roda sobresselente *nowη tayn-yoo roh-duh soh-* *bre-sseh-lent*
I don't have spare light bulbs	Não tenho lâmpadas *nowη tayn-yoo lam-puh-duhsh*
I've run out of petrol	Estou sem gasolina *shtoh saymη gah-soh-lee-nuh*
Have you got a petrol can?	Tem uma lata de gasolina? *taymη oo-muh lah-tuh duh* *gah-soh-lee-nuh?*
My car won't start	O meu carro não pega *oo may-oo kah-roo nowη pay-* *guh*
There's a funny noise	Há um barulho estranho *ah oomη bah-rul-yoo shtran-yoo*

Could you change the wheel?	Podia mudar a roda? *po-<u>dee</u>-yuh moo-<u>dar</u> uh <u>roh</u>-duh?*
The engine has overheated	O motor aqueceu demais *oo moh-<u>tor</u> a-kuh-<u>say</u>-oo deh-<u>mysh</u>*
How long will it take?	Quanto tempo leva? *<u>kwan</u>-too <u>tem</u>-poo <u>lay</u>-vuh?*
It's urgent	É urgente *eh ur-<u>zhent</u>*
I'm/We're...	Estou/Estamos... *shtoh/<u>shta</u>-moosh...*
...(5) kilometres away	...a (5) quilómetros *...uh (<u>sin</u>-koo) kee-<u>lo</u>-me-troosh*
...on the (Lisbon) road	...na estrada de (Lisboa) *...nuh <u>shtra</u>-duh duh (lizh-<u>bo</u>-uh)*
...before exit 30	...antes da saída 30 *...<u>an</u>-tuhsh duh sy-<u>ee</u>-duh <u>trin</u>-tuh*
It's a (Fiat) car	É um (Fiat) *eh oomη (Fiat)*
It's (blue)	É (azul) *eh (a-<u>zool</u>)*
The registration number is...	A matrícula é... *uh mah-<u>tree</u>-ku-luh eh...*

For numbers see page 183. For colours see page 156.

Can you...?	Pode...? *pod...?*
...help me	...ajudar-me *...a-zhoo-<u>dar</u>-muh*
...take me to (a petrol station)	...levar-me a (uma estação de serviço) *...luh-<u>var</u>-muh uh (<u>oo</u>-muh shta-<u>ssown</u>η duh sair-<u>vee</u>-ssoo)*

...send a mechanic	...mandar um mecánico ...man-_dar_ oomη meh-_kah_-nee-koo
...send a breakdown lorry/service	...mandar um pronto socorro ...man-_dar_ oomη _pron_-too soh-_koh_-roo
...give me a lift	...dar-me uma boleia ..._dar_-muh _oo_-muh boh-_lay_-uh
...call an ambulance	...chamar uma ambulância ...sha-_mar_ _oo_-muh am-boo-_lan_-see-yuh
Do you do repairs?	Fazem reparos? _fa_-zaymη reh-_pah_-roosh?
I don't know what is wrong with it	Não sei qual é o problema nowη say kwal eh oo pro-_blay_-muh
The...is broken/doesn't work	...está estragado/a/não funciona ...shta shtra-_gah_-doo/uh/nowη fun-ssee-_oh_-nuh
...windscreen	...o pára-brisas ...oo _pa_-ruh-_bree_-suhsh
...seatbelt	...o cinto de segurança ...oo _sin_-too duh seh-goo-_ran_-ssuh
...wing mirror	...o espelho exterior ...oo _shpel_-yoo shteh-ree-_yor_
...rear light	...a luz da retaguarda ...uh loozh duh re-tuh-_gwa_-duh
Can you check...?	Pode verificar...? pod veh-ree-fee-_kar_...?
...the accelerator	...o acelerador ...oo a-sel-er-a-_dor_
...the brakes	...os travões ...oosh _tra-voyη_sh

...the carburettor	...o carburador ...*oo kar-boo-ra-<u>dor</u>*
...the clutch	...o pedal de embriagagem ...*oo peh-<u>dal</u> duh em-bree-a-ga-zhaymη*
...the engine	...o motor ...*oo moh-<u>tor</u>*
...the exhaust pipe	...o tubo de escape ...*oo <u>too</u>-boo duh shcap*
...the fan belt	...a correia da ventoinha ...*uh koh-<u>ray</u>-uh duh ven-toh-<u>een</u>-yuh*
...the gear box	...a caixa de velocidades ...*uh <u>kye</u>-shuh duh veh-loh-see-<u>dah</u>-desh*
...the handbrake	...o travão de mão ...*oo tra-<u>vown</u> duh mown*
...the indicators	...os piscas-piscas ...*oosh <u>pish</u>-kuhsh-<u>pish</u>-kuhsh*
...the petrol pump	...a bomba de gasolina ...*uh <u>bom</u>-buh duh gah-soh-<u>lee</u>-nuh*
...the spark plugs	...as velas ...*uhsh <u>vay</u>-luhsh*
...the starter (motor)	...o motor de arranque ...*oo moh-<u>tor</u> duh a-<u>rank</u>*
...the steering	...a direcção ...*uh dee-reh-<u>ssown</u>*
...the suspension	...a suspensão ...*uh suss-pen-<u>sown</u>*
When will (the car) be ready?	Quando estará pronto (o carro)? *<u>kwan</u>-doo shta-<u>ra</u> <u>pron</u>-too (oo <u>kah</u>-roo)?*

This is the key...	Esta é a chave...
	eh-shtuh eh uh shav...
...to the boot	...da mala
	...duh ma-luh
...to the petrol tank	...do depósito
	...doo duh-poh-see-too
Could you give me an estimate/ bill?	Podia dar-me um orçamento/ uma factura?
	po-dee-yuh dar-muh oomη or-ssa-men-too/oo-muh fak-too-ruh?
Is VAT included?	Está incluído o IVA?
	shta in-kloo-ee-doo oo ee-vuh?
Here are the documents	Aqui tem os documentos
	a-key taymη oosh doh-ku-men-toosh

You may hear:

Onde está?	Where are you?
ond shta?	
Qual é o problema?	What is the problem?
kwal eh oo pro-blay-muh?	
Qual é a marca do carro?	What make of car is it?
kwal eh uh mar-kuh doo kah-roo?	
Tem de deixá-lo...	You must leave it...
taymη duh day-sha-loo...	
...até amanhã	...until tomorrow
...uh-tay uh-mun-yaη	
...três dias	...for three days
...traysh dee-yuhsh	
Tem os seus documentos, por favor?	Do you have your documents, please?
taymη oosh say-yoosh doh-ku-men-toosh, por fa-vor?	

Será difícil reparar	It'll be difficult to repair
se-ra dee-fee-seel re-puh-rar	
Sinto muito, mas virou sucata	I'm afraid it's a write-off
sin-too mween-too, msh vee-roh	
su-ka-tuh	

ROAD TRAVEL

You may see:

Bemvindos a...	Welcome to...
Circule pela esquerda/direita	Keep left/right
Cruzamento (perigoso)	(dangerous) Crossroads
Cuidado	Caution
Curva perigosa	Dangerous bend
Dê passagem	Give way
Desvio	Diversion
Devagar	Slow
Estacionamento proibido	No parking
Obras	Roadworks
Passagem de nível	Level crossing
Perigo	Danger
Perigo de incêndio	Danger of fire
Portagem	Toll
Se beber não conduza	Don't drink and drive
Sentido único	One-way
Velocidade máxima	Maximum speed
Via de acesso	Access only

BUYING TICKETS – AIR

Is there a flight to (Madeira)?	Há um voo para (a Madeira)? *ah oomη voh puh-ruh (uh Mah-day-ruh)?*
A ticket for (Manchester), please	Um bilhete para (Manchester), por favor *oomη bil-yet puh-ruh (Manchester) por fa-vor*
Do I/we have to make a connection?	Tenho/Temos de fazer ligação? *tayn-yoo/tay-moosh duh fa-zair lee-ga-ssowη?*
When do I/we have to check in?	A que horas tenho/temos de fazer o check-in? *uh kay or-ush tayn-yoo/tay-moosh duh fa-zair oo check-in?*
I/we want to...my/our flight	Quero/Queremos...o meu/nosso voo *kair-oo/kuh-ray-moosh...oo may-oo/noh-ssoo voh*
...confirm	...confirmar *...con-feer-mar*
...cancel	...cancelar *...can-se-lar*
...change	...trocar *...tro-kar*
Where is...?	Onde é...? *ond eh...?*
...the (TAP) counter	...o balcão (da TAP) *...oo bal-kowη (duh TAP)*
...the duty-free shop	...a loja de duty-free *...uh lo-zhuh duh duty-free*
...the café	...o café *...oo kah-fay*

Is it delayed?	Está atrasado? *shta a-tra-sa-doo?*
How much is it delayed?	Quanto tempo é que está atrasado? *kwan-too tem-poo eh kuh shta a-tra-sa-doo?*
I've missed my plane	Perdi o voo *per-dee oo voh*
When is the next flight to...?	Quando é o próximo voo para...? *kwan-doo eh oo pro-see-moo voh puh-ruh...?*
I've lost my passport	Perdi o meu passaporte *per-dee oo may-oo pass-uh-port*
Which is the queue for...?	Qual é a bicha para...? *kwal eh uh bee-shuh puh-ruh...?*

RAIL

The Portuguese rail network is relatively small but cheap and very efficient, with some up-to-date high-speed trains. The types of train you may use are:

High-speed Alfa-Pendular (Lisbon to Porto and the north)

Rápido Intercidades (IC)	Inter-city
Regional and inter-regional	
Suburbano	Suburban lines, many on commuter routes
International routes	For example, the luxury Lusitânia Comboio Hotel (hotel train) to Madrid or the Sud-Expresso through Spain and France

There are various discount tariffs, including: groups, young people (*Cartão Jovem*), those accompanying disabled people, children (under 4s travel free, 4–12 at half-fare), over 65s, and family travel cards. There are also different types of passes and multi-journey tickets –

information is available at stations and tourist information offices. You can book tickets for the Alfa and Rápido trains in advance, but whatever train you are taking, you must have a ticket before boarding. In cases where you board at an unstaffed or closed station, there should be a ticket collector on board who will sell you a ticket. Second class travel is of a good enough standard and first class is better value than you might expect, although there is usually no need to use it.

If you intend to purchase your ticket by card, you must inform the clerk as you request it as it is a different transaction to cash. It may not be possible to pay this way in small, rural stations.

AT THE STATION

Do you have...?	Tem...? *taymη...?*
...a (railway) timetable	...um horário (de comboios) *...oomη or-rah-ree-yoo (duh com-boy-oosh)*
...information about discounts	...informações sobre descontos *...in-for-ma-soyηsh so-bray desh-con-toosh*
How many trains are there for (Lisbon)...?	Quantos comboios há para (Lisboa)...? *kwan-toosh com-boy-oosh ah puh-ruh (lizh-bo-uh)...?*
...today	...hoje *...ozh*
...tomorrow	...amanhã *...uh-mun-yaη*
...on Saturday	...no Sábado *...noo sa-ba-doo*
What time does...leave?	A que horas parte...? *uh kay or-uhsh part...?*

...the next train	...o próximo comboio
	...oo pro-see-moo com-boy-oo
...the first train	...o primeiro comboio
	...oo pree-may-roo com-boy-oo
...the last train	...o último comboio
	...oo ul-tee-moo com-boy-oo
Does it stop at all the stations?	Pára em todas as estações?
	pa-ruh aymη toh-doosh uhsh shta-ssoyηsh?
Do I have to change trains/ make a connection?	Tenho de mudar/fazer ligação?
	tayη-yoo duh moo-dar/fa-zair lee-ga-ssowη?
How long does it take?	Quanto tempo leva?
	kwan-too tem-poo lay-vuh?
When does it arrive?	A que horas chega?
	uh kay or-uhsh shay-guh?
From which platform does it leave?	Parte de que linha?
	part duh kuh leen-yuh?
Is it delayed?	Está atrasado?
	shta a-tra-sa-doo?
Is/are there...?	Há...?
	ah...?
...a bar	...um bar
	...oomη bar
...couchettes	...couchettes
	...koo-shet-esh
...a restaurant car	...restaurante
	...rush-to-rant
...sleeping compartments	...camas
	...ka-muhsh
At what time does the bar open/ close?	A que horas abre/fecha o bar?
	uh kay or-uhsh a-bray/fay-shuh oo bar?

Where is...?	Onde é...?
	ond eh...?
...the left-luggage office	...o depósito de bagagens
	...oo duh-<u>poh</u>-see-too duh ba-<u>ga</u>-zhaynsh
...the platform	...a linha/plataforma
	...uh <u>leen</u>-yuh/pla-tuh-<u>for</u>-muh
...the ticket window	...a bilheteira
	...uh bil-yuh-<u>tay</u>-ruh
...the waiting room	...a sala de espera
	...uh <u>sa</u>-luh duh <u>shpay</u>-ruh

BUYING TICKETS

Two tickets...	dois bilhetes...
	doysh bil-<u>yet</u>-ush
...to Faro	...para Faro
	...<u>puh</u>-ruh <u>fa</u>-roo
...for the two o'clock Alfa	...para o Alfa das duas horas
	...<u>puh</u>-ruh oo <u>al</u>-fuh duhsh <u>doo</u>-uhsh <u>or</u>-uhsh
Can I reserve a seat?	Posso reservar um lugar?
	<u>poh</u>-ssoo re-sair-<u>var</u> oomη loo-<u>gar</u>?
Do you have to book in advance?	É preciso reservar com antecedência?
	eh pruh-<u>see</u>-soo re-sair-<u>var</u> comη an-teh-se-<u>den</u>-see-yuh?
Is there a discount for...?	Há desconto para...?
	ah desh-<u>con</u>-too <u>puh</u>-ruh...?
...children	...crianças
	...cree-<u>yan</u>-suhsh
...students	...estudantes
	...shtoo-<u>dan</u>-tush

...retired people	...os idosos/a terceira idade ...*oosh ee-<u>doh</u>-soosh/uh tair-<u>say</u>-ruh ee-<u>dad</u>*
A...ticket, please	um bilhete...se faz favor *oomη bil-<u>yet</u>...suh fash fa-<u>vor</u>*
single	simples/de ida *<u>sim</u>-plesh/duh <u>ee</u>-duh*
return	de ida e volta *duh <u>ee</u>-duh ee <u>vol</u>-tuh*
first/second class	de primeira/segunda classe *duh pree-<u>may</u>-ruh/se-<u>gun</u>-duh class*
smoking	fumador *foo-muh-<u>dor</u>*
non-smoking	não-fumador *<u>nown</u>-foo-muh-<u>dor</u>*
and one child (half)	e um meio *ee oomη <u>may</u>-oo*
How much is that?	Quanto é? *<u>kwan</u>-too eh?*
Could you write it down?	Podia escrevê-lo? *po-<u>dee</u>-yuh shcre-<u>vay</u>-loo?*
Can I pay by credit card?	Posso pagar com cartão de crédito? *<u>poh</u>-ssoo <u>puh</u>-gar comη kar-<u>town</u> duh <u>cre</u>-dee-too?*
Does it carry bicycles?	Transporta bicicletas? *trans-<u>por</u>-tuh bee-see-<u>klay</u>-tuhsh?*

LUGGAGE

I would like...	Queria... *<u>kree</u>-uh...*
...to leave this	...deixar isto *...day-<u>shar</u> <u>ish</u>-too*

Could you help me with my luggage?	Podia ajudar-me com a bagagem? *po-<u>dee</u>-yuh a-zhoo-<u>dar</u>-muh comη uh buh-<u>ga</u>-zhaymη?*

ON THE TRAIN

Is this...?	Este/Esta é...? *esht/<u>eh</u>-shtuh eh...?*
...the train for (Lagos)	...o comboio para (Lagos) *...oo com-<u>boy</u>-oo <u>puh</u>-ruh (<u>la</u>-goosh)*
...the platform for (Tavira)	...a linha para (Tavira) *...uh <u>leen</u>-yuh <u>puh</u>-ruh (ta-<u>vee</u>-ruh)*
...the second class carriage?	...o vagão/a carruagem de segunda classe? *...oo va-<u>gown</u>/uh ka-roo-<u>a</u>-zhaymη duh se-<u>gun</u>-duh class?*
Which is the...carriage?	Qual é o vagão...? *kwal eh oo va-<u>gown</u>...?*
...first class	...de primeira classe *...duh pree-<u>may</u>-ruh class*
...restaurant	...restaurante *...rush-to-<u>rant</u>*
I don't have a reservation	Não reservei lugar *nowη re-sair-<u>vay</u> loo-<u>gar</u>*
Excuse me/I'm sorry	Desculpe... *desh-<u>koolp</u>...*
Is this seat taken?	(Este lugar) Está ocupado? *(esht loo-<u>gar</u>) shta oh-koo-<u>pa</u>-doo?*
Could you...?	Podia...? *po-<u>dee</u>-yuh...?*
...find me a seat	...procurar um lugar para mim *...pro-koo-<u>rar</u> oomη loo-<u>gar</u> <u>puh</u>-ruh meemη*

...tell me when we get to (Lisbon)	...avisar-me quando chegarmos a (Lisboa)
	...a-vee-_sar_-muh _kwan_-doo shuh-_gar_-moosh uh (lizh-_bo_-uh)
Have we arrived?	Já chegámos?
	zha shuh-_ga_-moosh?
This is my seat	Este é o meu lugar
	esht eh oo _may_-oo loo-_gar_
This seat is taken	(Este lugar) Está ocupado
	(esht loo-_gar_) shta oh-koo-_pa_-doo
Is the (Lisbon) train running late?	O comboio para (Lisboa) está atrasado?
	oo com-_boy_-oo _puh_-ruh (lizh-_bo_-uh) shta a-tra-_sa_-doo?

You may see:

1/2 classe	1ˢᵗ/2ⁿᵈ class
Bilheteira	Ticket office
Bilhetes para hoje	Tickets for immediate travel
Chegadas	Arrivals
CP – Caminhos de Ferro Portugueses	Portuguese Railways
Depósito de bagagens	Left luggage
Destino	Destination
Entrada	Entrance
Estação CF (Caminho de Ferro)	(railway) Station
Homens/Cavaleiros/WC	Men's toilet
Horário	Timetable
Informações	Information
Linha/Gare/Cais	Platform
Partidas	Departures
Saída	Exit

Senhoras/Damas/WC	Women's toilet
Sala de espera	Waiting room
Vagão	Carriage

You may hear:

Tem de mudar (em...) *taymη duh moo-dar (aymη...)*	You have to change (at...)
Tem um atraso de (meia hora) *taymη oomη a-tra-soo duh (may-uh or-uh)*	It's (half an hour) late
Há suplemento/taxa *ah su-plee-men-too/tah-shuh*	There is a supplementary charge
O comboio que vai entrar na linha número (5)... *oo com-boy-oo kuh vye en-trar nuh leen-yuh noo-muh-roo (sin-koo)...*	The train now arriving at platform (5)...
O comboio com destino a (Lisboa) vai entrar na linha número (3) *oo com-boy-oo comη desh-tee-noo uh (lizh-bo-uh) vye en-trar nuh leen-yuh noo-muh-roo (traysh)*	The train for (Lisbon) is arriving at platform (3)
O comboio procedente de (Aveiro) vai chegar dentro de (10) minutos *oo com-boy-oo proh-se-dent duh (uh-vay-roo) vye shuh-gar den-troo duh (desh) mee-noo-toosh*	The train from (Aveiro) will arrive in (10) minutes
Não há comboios hoje *nowη ah com-boy-oosh ozh*	There are no trains today
Há greve *Ah grehv*	There is a strike
Tem cartão de jovem? *taymη kar-town duh zho-vaymη?*	Do you have a student card?

Tem de sair em...
taymη duh sigh-eer aymη...

You have to get off at...

BY COACH

There is a good network of operators, including EVA, Rodonorte and
Rede Expressos, covering most of the country, including some quite
remote areas.
Eurolines run from London Victoria coach station to Portugal, via
France and Spain, and back.
The modern coaches are mostly very comfortable, efficient and cheap.
Coaches often depart from specified pick-up points in a town, rather
than at an official 'station'.
Often you can only buy single tickets for each leg of the journey.

Where is the bus/coach station?	Onde fica o terminal/central de camionagem/estação de camionetas? *ond fee-kuh oo tair-mee-nal/sen-tral duh ka-mee-oh-nah-zhaymη/shta-ssown duh ka-mee-oh-ne-tuhsh?*
When are there coaches to (Lisbon)?	Quando há camionetas para (Lisboa)? *kwan-doo ah ka-mee-oh-ne-tuhsh puh-ruh (lizh-bo-uh)?*
A ticket for (Lisbon)	Um bilhete para (Lisboa) *oomη bil-yet puh-ruh (lizh-bo-uh)*
by the window	à janela *a zha-nay-luh*
How do I get to...?	O que faço para ir a...? *oo kuh fa-ssoo puh-ruh eer uh...?*
What time does it leave/arrive?	A que horas parte/chega? *uh kay or-uhsh part/shay-guh?*

Where does it leave from?	De onde parte?
	duh ond part?
Does it have...?	tem...?
	taymη...?
...air conditioning	...ar condicionamento
	...ar con-dee-see-yon-a-<u>men</u>-too
...a toilet	...toilete/lavabo
	...twa-<u>let</u>/la-<u>va</u>-boo
Where does it stop?	Onde pára?
	ond <u>pa</u>-ruh?
Do I need to change?	Preciso de mudar?
	pruh-<u>see</u>-soo duh moo-<u>dar</u>?
How long will I need to wait there?	Quanto tempo é que lá tenho de esperar?
	<u>kwan</u>-too <u>tem</u>-poo eh kuh la <u>tayn</u>-yoo duh <u>shpe</u>-rar?
How long do we stop here?	Por quanto tempo ficamos aqui?
	por <u>kwan</u>-too <u>tem</u>-poo fee-<u>ka</u>-moosh a-<u>key</u>?

BY BUS, UNDERGROUND AND FUNICULAR (LISBON)

The main operator for transport in Lisbon is CARRIS.

In Lisbon, buses, trams and the funiculars all use the same tickets, which can be bought as you board or as discounted multi-journey tickets from CARRIS kiosks.

Special travel cards are available in Lisbon, Porto and other main cities, including the useful Lisboa Card, with access to transport and places of interest.

Underground tickets can be purchased at the metro stations, including from automatic machines.

For all transport you must make sure your ticket is validated – either through a machine on board (*obliterador*), or through automatic barriers at the stations.

On most buses you enter at the front and leave through doors in the middle – watch what other people do!

Could you give me...?	Podia dar-me...? *po-dee-yuh dar-muh...?*
...a book of tickets	...uma caderneta de módulos *...oo-muh ka-duh-ne-tuh duh moh-doo-loosh*
...a (bus) pass	...um passe *...oomη pass*
...a tourist travel card	...um passe turístico *...oomη pass too-rish-tee-koo*
...a monthly ticket	...um passe mensal *...oomη pass men-sal*
(One) to (the centre), please	(Um) para (o centro), por favor *(oomη) puh-ruh (oo sen-troo), por fa-vor*
Is this the stop for the number 7 bus?	Esta é a paragem para o autocarro número 7? *eh-shtuh eh uh puh-ra-zhemη puh-ruh oo ow-too-karr-oo noo-muh-roo set?*
Does this bus go (to the centre)?	Este autocarro vai (ao centro)? *esht ow-too-karr-oo vye (ow sen-troo)?*
Do you go through (Alfama)?	Passa por (Alfama)? *pa-ssuh por (al-fam-uh)?*
Do you have a map...?	Tem um mapa...? *taymη oomη ma-puh...?*
...of the underground	...do metro *...doo meh-troo*
...of the bus routes	...dos itinerários dos autocarros *...doosh ee-tee-nuh-ra-ree-yoosh doosh ow-too-karr-oosh*

Do you have a timetable?	Tem um horário?
	taymη oomη or-rah-ree-yoo?
Which line should I take to go to (Oriente) station?	Qual linha devo tomar para a estação Oriente?
	kwal leen-yuh day-voo toh-mar puh-ruh uh shta-ssown o-ree-ent?
Do I have to change?	Tenho de mudar?
	tayn-yoo duh moo-dar?
Where?	Onde?
	ond?
Could you let me know when to get off (for…)?	Podia avisar-me quando devo sair (para…)?
	po-dee-yuh a-vee-sar-muh kwan-doo day-voo sigh-eer (puh-ruh…)?
How long does it take?	Quanto tempo leva?
	kwan-too tem-poo lay-vuh?

You may see:

Lotação…lugares de pé/sentados	Limit…standing/seated
Multa	Fine
Pague ao motorista	Pay the driver
Parar	Stopping
Proibido fumar	No smoking
Reservados a deficientes físicos, grávidas e acompanhantes de crianças de colo	Reserved for the disabled, pregnant women, and those with small children
Válido só depois de obliterado	Valid only after 'validating' (in machine)
Verifique o troco no acto de pagamento	Check your change as you pay

CAR HIRE

Airports have most of the main car-hire firms represented, as do many towns in the Algarve and the larger cities.

Tariffs and conditions of hire are widely available in English.

You need to be 23 years old and have been driving for one year to hire a car in Portugal.

I've booked a car...	Tenho um automóvel reservado *tayn-yoo oomη ow-too-moh-vel re-sair-va-doo*
My name is...	O meu nome é... *oo may-oo nom eh...*
I'd like to hire a small/large car	Queria alugar um automóvel pequeno/grande *kree-uh a-loo-gar oomη ow-too-moh-vel pe-kay-noo/grand*
For today/one week	Para hoje/uma semana *puh-ruh ozh/oo-muh suh-mah-nuh*
How much is the daily charge/ per kilometre?	Quanto custa por dia/por quilómetro? *kwan-too cush-tuh por dee-yuh/por kee-lo-me-troo?*
Is insurance included?	O seguro está incluído? *oo se-goo-roo shta in-kloo-ee-doo?*
Can I leave it in (Lisbon)?	Posso deixá-lo em (Lisboa)? *poh-ssoo day-sha-loo aymη (lizh-boh-uh)?*
Do you want to see my driving licence?	Quer ver a minha carta de condução? *kair vair uh meen-yuh car-tuh duh con-doo-ssown?*

TAXIS

Taxis display a green light if they are occupied. Sometimes, two lights are lit – this signifies a higher tariff, e.g. at weekends. When the central light is on, the taxi is available for hire.

Taxi travel is generally very cheap, but fares rise after 10pm and at weekends and bank holidays.

Airport information desks can issue a tariff rate of approximate fares from the airport to main towns, so you have an idea of price before you set off.

Some charge extra for luggage – and not all taxi drivers help you load it in!

Taxis can be found in various obvious locations, can be flagged down in the street or called from a taxi firm.

Taxi!	Táxi! _tax-ee!_
Could you take me...?	Podia levar-me...? _po-dee-yuh luh-var-muh...?_
To...please	Para...por favor _puh-ruh...por fa-vor_
...here (indicating somewhere)	...aqui _...a-key_
...to this address	...a esta morada _...uh eh-shtuh mo-ra-duh_
...to the airport	...ao aeroporto _...ow eh-ro-por-too_
...to the hotel (Portimar)	...ao hotel (Portimar) _...ow o-tel (portimar)_
How much is it to the city/the airport?	Quanto é para a cidade/o aeroporto? _kwan-too eh puh-ruh uh see-da-duh/oo eh-ro-por-too?_

Could you stop here, please?	Podia parar aqui, por favor?
	po-dee-yuh puh-rar a-key, por fa-vor?
Could you...?	Podia...?
	po-dee-yuh...?
...wait for me	...esperar-me
	...shpuh-rar-muh
...help me with my cases	...ajudar-me com as malas
	...a-zhoo-dar-muh comŋ uhsh mal-uhsh
I'm in a hurry	Estou com pressa
	shtoh comŋ press-uh
You can keep the change	Pode ficar com o troco
	pod fee-kar comŋ oo tro-koo

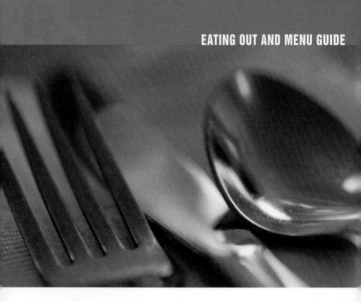

EATING OUT

The Portuguese love eating out and drinking in bars, cafés and restaurants – it is a fundamental part of life there, and very enjoyable too.

You can get snacks and drinks all day in cafés and café-bars, often from breakfast-time onwards, when the Portuguese will call in for a strong coffee and a cake on the way to work. Restaurants serve lunches from around midday until 2.30/3pm, and evening meals from about 7pm until late.

Children are welcome in all eating establishments, and it is not uncommon to see Portuguese children out with their families until quite late in the evening. They are usually very well-behaved!

Cheap eating places, known as *tascas*, are frequented by the Portuguese, where you can get a good, cheap wholesome meal

– you may have to ask around to find one. At the other extreme, in many cities you will find expensive top-of-the-range eateries, including *marisqueiras*, which specialise in seafood.

International cuisine is fairly widespread in larger towns, the most popular being Chinese, African or Brazilian.

Fast food has also made an impact in Portugal, and today you will find burger joints and pizza parlours in many places.

In ordinary restaurants, the tourist set menu, *ementa turística*, is often good value, and saves having to try to decide from an extensive menu.

Tables are usually set with an array of tempting nibbles, which form part of the cover charge, or *couvert*. Just be careful with plates of smoked ham or prawns – often these are charged extra and can be pricey. If you do not want any of the nibbles, tell your waiter at the start, as you will be charged for the whole plate if you so much as try a little of it.

A tip is discretionary as service is generally included (*serviço incluído*) and *IVA incluído* means VAT is also included.

In most bars and cafés you pay when you have finished, but at some canteen-style places in airports you have to pay at the cash till when you order, so you need to know in advance what you want.

Some restaurants price the food by weight – you simply help yourself to whatever you want from a display range and the plateful is weighed when you pay. This is known as *comida a peso*.

You may see:

Adega	Wine cellar
Almoços	Lunches
(ao) Balcão	(at the) Bar/Counter
Bar	Bar
Café/cafetaria	Café
Casa de chá	Tea shop
Cervejaria	Beer cellar

Churrasqueira	Barbecue/steak house
Comida a peso	Food sold by weight
Ementa turística	Tourist menu
Esplanada	Pavement café
Jantares	Dinners
Lanches	Snacks
Lanchonete	Snack bar
Marisqueira	Seafood restaurant
Pastelaria	Cake/Coffee shop
Refeições ligeiras	Light meals/snacks
Restaurante	Restaurant
Tasca/tasquinha	Cheap eating place

RESERVATIONS

I'd like to reserve a table for...	Queria reservar uma mesa para... *kree-uh re-sair-var oo-muh may-suh puh-ruh...*
...two	...dois *...doysh*
...eight o'clock	...as oito horas *...ush oy-too or-uhsh*
...tonight	...esta noite *...eh-shtuh noyt*
...tomorrow	...amanhã *...uh-mun-yan*
I/We have a table reserved in the name of	Tenho/Temos uma mesa reservada em nome de... *tayn-yoo/tay-moosh oo-muh may-suh ruh-sair-va-duh aymη nom duh...*
Do you have any tables free?	Tem uma mesa livre? *taymη oo-muh may-suh lee-vruh?*

I prefer that one	Prefiro aquela *pruh-fee-roo a-ke-luh*
By the window	perto da janela *per-too duh zha-nay-luh*
At the back	ao fundo *ow fun-doo*
Outside/on the terrace	fora/no terraço *for-uh/noo te-rah-ssoo*
In the corner	no canto *noo can-too*
There are four of us	Somos quatro *soh-moosh kwa-troo*

You may hear:

Reservaram mesa?
reh-sair-vah-rown may-suh?

Have you reserved a table?

Não há mesas neste momento
nown ah may-suhsh nesht mo-men-too

There aren't any tables free
at the moment

Para quantas pessoas?
puh-ruh kwan-tuhsh pe-ssoh-uhsh?

For how many people?

Terão de esperar/voltar
teh-rown duh shpe-rar/vol-tar

You will have to wait/come back

Haverá uma mesa dentro de
(20) minutos
*av-er-ra oo-muh may-suh den-troo
duh (vint) mee-noo-toosh*

There'll be a table free in
(20) minutes

Por aqui
por a-key

This way

Temos esta ou aquela
tay-moosh eh-shtuh oh a-ke-luh

We have this one or that one

ORDERING

Excuse me (to call waiter/ waitress)	Faz favor! *fash fa-vor!*
I'd/We'd like...	Queria/Queríamos... *kree-uh/kree-uh-moosh...*
...a cup of...	uma chávena de *oo-muh sha-vuh-nuh duh*
...a glass of...	um copo de *oomη koh-poo duh*
...a bottle of...	uma garrafa de *oo-muh guh-ra-fuh duh*
...a jug of...	um jarro de *oomη zha-roo duh*
...half a bottle	meia garrafa *may-uh guh-ra-fuh*
...a can/tin	uma lata *oo-muh lah-tuh*
I'd/We'd like...	Queria/Queríamos... *kree-uh/kree-uh-moosh...*
...the menu	...a lista/a ementa *...uh lish-tuh/uh ay-men-tuh*
...the menu of the day	...a ementa do dia *...uh ay-men-tuh doo dee-yuh*
...the tourist menu	...a ementa turística *...uh ay-men-tuh too-rish-tee-kuh*
...a typical local dish	...um prato típico de aqui *...oomη pra-too ti-pee-koo duh a-key*
...something vegetarian	...um prato vegetariano *...oomη pra-too veh-zhee-tah-ree-yah-noo*
...the wine list	...a lista dos vinhos *...uh lish-tuh doosh vin-yoosh*

...a half portion	...meia dose ..._may_-uh dohz
Do you have a children's menu?	Tem uma lista para crianças? taymη _oo_-muh _lish_-tuh _puh_-ruh cree-_yaη_-suhsh?
Do you serve...?	Servem...? _sair_-vaymη...?
What do you recommend?	O que recomenda? oo kuh reh-coh-_men_-duh?
What is (this)?	O que é (isto)? oo key eh (_eesh_-too)?
What's...like?	Como é...? _com_-oo eh...?
What does it have in it?	O que é que tem dentro? oo key eh kuh taymη _den_-troo?
Does it have meat/fish in it?	Isto tem carne/peixe? _eesh_-too taymη karn/paysh?
What does it come with?	Vem com que? vaymη comη kay?
We haven't chosen yet	Ainda não escolhemos ay-_in_-duh nowη shcol-_ay_-moosh
Could you bring...?	podia trazer...? po-_dee_-yuh tra-_zair_...?
...some bread	...pão ...powη
...butter	...manteiga ...man-_tay_-guh
...pepper	...pimenta ...pee-_men_-tuh
...salt	...sal ...sal
...sugar	...açúcar ...a-_ssoo_-kar

...water	...água ..._a_-gwa
...a fork	...um garfo ...oomη _gar_-foo
...a knife	...uma faca ..._oo_-muh _fah_-kuh
...a (soup/dessert/tea)spoon	...uma colher (de sopa/ sobremesa/café) ..._oo_-muh kuhl-_yair_ (duh _soh_-puh/soh-bree-_may_-suh/kah-_fay_)
...a glass	...um copo ...oomη _koh_-poo
...a serviette/napkin	...um guardanapo ...oomη gwar-duh-_na_-poo
...an ashtray	...um cinzeiro ...oomη sin-_zay_-roo
...toothpicks	...palitos ...pah-_lee_-toosh
For starters...	Para começar... _puh_-ruh coh-muh-_ssar_...
Then/Next...	Depois... de-_poysh_...
For the main course...	Para o prato principal... _puh_-ruh oo _pra_-too prin-see-_pal_...
For dessert...	Para sobremesa... _puh_-ruh soh-bree-_may_-suh...
For my husband/wife...	Para o meu marido/a minha mulher _puh_-ruh oo _may_-oo mah-_ree_-doo/uh _meen_-yuh mul-_yair_
That's enough, thank you	Chega, obrigado/a _shay_-guh, oh-bree-_gah_-doo/uh
Is a half-portion enough for one person?	Meia dose dá para uma pessoa? _may_-uh dohz dah _puh_-ruh _oo_-muh peh-_ssoh_-uh?

Cheers!	Saúde! *sa-<u>ood</u>!*
Same again, please	O mesmo, por favor *oo <u>mezh</u>-moo, por fa-<u>vor</u>*
Another one	Mais um/uma, se faz favor *mysh oomη/<u>oo</u>-muh, suh fash fa-<u>vor</u>*

You may hear:

Recomendo... *reh-coh-<u>men</u>-doo...*	I recommend...
Já não há *zha nowη ah*	There is none left
O/A...está muito bom/boa hoje *oo/uh...shta <u>mwee</u>η-too bomη/<u>boh</u>-uh ozh*	The...is very good today
Posso sugerir...? *<u>poh</u>-ssoo soo-zheh-<u>reer</u>...?*	May I suggest...?
Só servimos almoços a partir do meio-dia *soh sair-<u>vee</u>-moosh al-<u>moh</u>-ssoosh uh par-<u>teer</u> doo <u>may</u>-oo-<u>dee</u>-yuh*	We only serve lunch from midday
Já escolheram? *zha shcol-<u>yair</u>-rowη?*	Have you chosen yet?
O que vão tomar? *oo kuh vowη toh-<u>mar</u>?*	What are you going to have?
Vão querer sobremesa? *vowη kuh-<u>rair</u> soh-bree-<u>may</u>-suh?*	Will you want dessert?
Para beber? *<u>puh</u>-ruh buh-<u>bair</u>?*	Any drinks?
Café? *kah-<u>fay</u>?*	Coffee?
Bom apetite/Bom proveito *bomη a-puh-<u>teet</u>/bomη pro- <u>vay</u>-too*	Bon appétit!

Gostaram?
gosh-tar-rown?

Did you enjoy it?

PROBLEMS AND QUERIES

Where is the toilet?

Onde é a casa de banho?
ond eh uh ka-suh duh ban-yoo?

Do you have a phone here?

Há telefone?
ah te-le-fon?

Is the (soup) on its way?

(A sopa) já vem?
(uh soh-puh) zha vaymη?

Will it be much longer?

Demora mais tempo?
deh-mor-uh mysh tem-poo?

I didn't ask for this

Não pedi isto
nowη peh-dee eesh-too

This isn't for me

Isto não é para mim
*eesh-too nowη eh puh-ruh
meemη*

Could you heat it a bit more?

Podia aquecê-lo um pouco mais?
*po-dee-yuh a-kay-say-loo oomη
poh-koo mysh?*

It's a bit...

Está um pouco...
shta oomη poh-koo...

...cold

...frio
...free-oo

...underdone

...cru/mal cozinhado
...kroo/mal coh-zeen-yah-doo

...overdone

...passado demais
...pah-ssah-doo deh-mysh

...salty

...salgado
...sal-gah-doo

There's a dish missing

Falta um prato
fal-tuh oomη pra-too

PAYING THE BILL

The bill, please	A conta, se faz favor *Uh con-tuh suh fash fa-vor*
I think there is a mistake	Creio que há um erro *cray-oo kuh ah oom̩ eh-roo*
We didn't have that	Não comemos isso *now̩ coh-may-moosh ee-ssoo*
What is this here?	O que é isto aqui? *oo kay eh eesh-too a-key?*
Can we have separate bills please?	Faça-nos contas separadas se faz favor *fa-ssuh-noosh con-tuhsh se-puh-rah-duhsh suh fash fa-vor*
All together	Tudo junto *too-doo zhun-too*
Is service included?	O serviço está incluído? *oo sair-vee-ssoo shta in-kloo-ee-doo?*
Keep the change	Fique com o troco *feek com̩ oo tro-koo*
We really enjoyed it	Gostámos muito *gosh-tah-moosh mwee̩-too*

DRINKS

COFFEES

Strong, black, small espresso	Um café/Uma bica *oom̩ kah-fay/oo-muh bee-kuh*
Weaker, small espresso	Um carioca *oom̩ kah-ree-oh-kuh*
Stronger espresso	Uma italiana *oo-muh ee-ta-lee-yah-nuh*
Large espresso	Um café duplo *oom̩ kah-fay doo-ploo*

Small white	Um garoto *oomη gah-<u>ro</u>-too*
Small, with just drop of milk	Um pingado *oomη pin-<u>gah</u>-doo*
Large white coffee	Um café com leite *oomη kah-<u>fay</u> comη layt*
Large half milk/half coffee	Uma meia de leite *<u>oo</u>-muh <u>may</u>-uh duh layt*
Milky coffee served in a glass	Um galão *oomη ga-<u>lown</u>*
Coffee with drop of firewater (brandy spirit)	Um cheirinho *oomη shay-<u>reen</u>-yoo*

OTHER NON-ALCOHOLIC DRINKS

Tea (with milk/lemon)	Um chá (com leite/limão) *oomη sha (comη layt/li-<u>mown</u>)*
Glass of milk...	Um copo de leite *oomη <u>koh</u>-poo duh layt*
...hot/cold	...quente/frio *...kent/<u>free</u>-oo*
(strawberry) Milkshake	Um batido (de morango) *oomη bah-<u>tee</u>-doo (duh moh-<u>ran</u>-goo)*
Fizzy/Still mineral water...	Uma água mineral com/sem gás *<u>oo</u>-muh <u>a</u>-gwa mi-ne-<u>ral</u> comη/saymη gash*
...cooled/room temperature	...fresco/natural *...<u>fresh</u>-koo/na-too-<u>ral</u>*
Coca Cola	Uma Coca Cola *<u>oo</u>-muh <u>koh</u>-kuh <u>koh</u>-luh*
Lemonade/Lemon drink	Uma limonada *<u>oo</u>-muh li-moh-<u>na</u>-duh*

Orange drink	Uma laranjada _oo_-muh la-ran-_zha_-duh
Tonic water	Uma água tónica _oo_-muh _a_-gwa _toh_-nee-kuh
Soft drink	Uma refrigerante ..._oo_-muh reh-free-zher-_ant_
(lemon/orange) Sumol (soft drink)	Um Sumol de (limão/laranja) ...oom_η_ soo-_mol_ duh (li-_mown_/la-_ran_-zhuh)
a/an...juice	Um sumo de... oom_η_ _soo_-moo duh...
...orange (fresh)	...laranja (natural) ...la-_ran_-zhuh (na-too-_ral_)
...apple	...maçã ...mah-_ssaη_
...pineapple	...ananás ...a-na-_nash_
...grapefruit	...toranja ...toh-_ran_-zhuh
...tomato	...tomate ...toh-_mat_
...mango	...manga ...man-guh
...banana	...banana ...ba-_na_-nuh
...passion fruit	...maracujá ...mah-ra-koo-_zha_

BEER

Beer	Uma cerveja _oo_-muh sair-_vay_-zhuh
Draught lager (small)	Uma imperial/um fino (in the north) _oo_-muh im-peh-ree-_al_/oom_η_ _fee_-noo

Large beer	Uma caneca *oo-muh ka-<u>ne</u>-kuh*
Dark beer (mild)	Uma cerveja preta *<u>oo</u>-muh sair-<u>vay</u>-zhuh <u>pre</u>-tuh*

WINE

Red wine	Um vinho tinto *oomη <u>vin</u>-yoo <u>tin</u>-too*
White wine	Um vinho branco *oomη <u>vin</u>-yoo <u>bran</u>-koo*
Rosé wine	Um vinho rosé/rosado *oomη <u>vin</u>-yoo ro-<u>say</u>/ro-<u>sah</u>-doo*
House wine	Um vinho da casa *oomη <u>vin</u>-yoo duh <u>ka</u>-suh*
Port	Um vinho do Porto *oomη <u>vin</u>-yoo doo <u>por</u>-too*
Brandy/Cognac	Um conhaque *oomη con-<u>yak</u>*
Gin	Um gim *oomη zheemη*
Gin and tonic	Um gim tónico *oomη zheemη <u>toh</u>-nee-koo*
Rum	Um rum *oomη rumη*
Whisky...	Um uísque... *oomη weeshk...*
...with ice	...com gelo *...comη <u>zhe</u>-loo*
...with water	...com água *...comη <u>a</u>-gwa*
...with soda	...com soda *...comη <u>soh</u>-duh*
...neat/on its own	...puro *...<u>poo</u>-roo*

Sweet	Doce *doss*
Dry	Seco *se-koo*

SPECIALITY DRINKS

Vinho verde *vin-yoo verd*	'Green' (young) wine – red or white
Vinho maduro *vin-yoo ma-doo-roo*	Often served cold, rich red wine
Um moscatel *oomη mosh-ka-tel*	Sweet dessert wine from Setúbal
Licor beirão *li-kor bay-rowη*	Sweet liqueur
Amêndoa amarga/Amarguinha *a-men-doh-uh a-mar-guh/a-mar-ghin-yuh*	Bitter almond liqueur from the Algarve
Ginginha *zhin-zhin-yuh*	Strong cherry brandy from Lisbon
Aguardente *a-gwar-dent*	Brandy spirit
Bagaço/Bagaceira *bah-ga-soo/bah-ga-ssay-ruh*	Strong spirits (firewater)
Medronho *meh-drohn-yoo*	Firewater from wild strawberry
Caipirinha *kigh-pee-rin-yuh*	Brazilian firewater, with sugar and lime

SNACKS

A...sandwich, please	Uma sandes/uma sanduíche de..., se faz favor *oo-muh san-desh/oo-muh san-dweesh duh..., suh fash fa-vor*

...cheese	...queijo ...*kay-zhoo*
...ham	...fiambre ...*fee-am-bray*
...egg	...ovo ...*oh-voo*
...tuna	...atum ...*a-toomη*
...chicken	...galinha ...*ga-lin-yuh*
...meat	...carne ...*karn*
...cheese and ham	uma sandes mista *oo-muh san-desh mish-tuh*
Hamburger	Um hamburguer *oomη am-boor-gair*
Hot dog	Um cachorro (quente) *oomη ka-shoh-roo (kent)*
Cheese/ham toasted sandwich	Uma tosta mista *oo-muh tosh-tuh mish-tuh*
Portion/two portions of...	Uma dose/duas doses de... *oo-muh dohz/doo-uhsh dohz-esh duh...*
Olives	Azeitonas *a-zay-toh-nuhsh*
Toast with butter	Torrada com manteiga *toh-ra-duh comη man-tay-guh*
Salty bean nibbles	Tremoços *tre-moh-ssoosh*
Cake	Um bolo *oomη boh-loo*
Pastry	Um pastel *oomη pash-tel*

(apple) Tart

Tarta de (maçã)
tar-tuh duh (mah-ssaŋ)

Slice of...

Uma fatia de...
oo-muh fah-tee-yuh duh...

WHAT'S ON THE MENU?

à...
ah

in the...style

à caçadora
ah ka-sa-dor-ruh

hunter-style

Acepipes/aperitivos
ah-suh-peepsh/ah-peh-ree-tee-voosh

appetisers

Acompanhamentos
ah-com-pan-yuh-men-toosh

side dishes

Açorda de alho
a-ssor-duh duh al-yoo

bread soup with garlic and egg

Açorda de marisco
a-ssor-duh duh ma-rish-koo

seafood mixture

Albardado
al-bar-dah-doo

in batter

A lista/ementa
uh leesh-tuh/ay-men-tuh

menu

à moda da casa
ah moh-duh duh ka-suh

house-style (house speciality)

à portuguesa
ah por-too-gay-suh

Portuguese style (with
tomatoes, wine/garlic)

ao forno
ow for-noo

oven-baked

Arroz (de ervilhas/tomate)
a-rozh (duh er-vil-yuhsh/toh-mat)

rice (with peas/tomatoes)

Arroz de marisco
a-rozh duh ma-rish-koo

seafood rice

Arroz de pato
a-rozh duh pa-too

duck rice

Arroz doce *a-rozh doss*	sweet rice pudding (cold)
Assado *a-ssa-doo*	roasted
Azeitonas *a-zay-toh-nuhsh*	olives
Bacalhau à Brás *ba-kal-yowu ah brash*	salted cod and potatoes
Bacalhau à Gomes de Sá *ba-kal-yowu ah gomsh duh sah*	salted cod with potatoes and eggs
Bacalhau à Zé Pipo *ba-kal-yowu ah zay pee-poo*	salted cod with mashed potatoes
Batatas cozidas *ba-ta-tuhsh coh-zee-duhsh*	boiled potatoes
Batatas fritas *ba-ta-tuhsh free-tuhsh*	chips/fries
Bebidas *buh-bee-duhsh*	drinks
Bem passado *baymη pah-ssah-doo*	well done
Bifana *bee-fa-nuh*	hot pork sandwich
Bife à cavalo/bitoque *beef ah ka-va-loo/bee-tok*	steak with fried egg
Bola de Berlim *boh-luh duh ber-limη*	custard-filled doughnut
Bolinho de bacalhau *boh-leen-yoo duh ba-kal-yowu*	potato/fish cakes
c/ = com *comη*	with...
Cabrito assado *ka-bree-too a-ssa-doo*	roast kid
Caldeirada *cal-day-ra-duh*	fish stew

Caldo verde
cal-doo verd
shredded kale soup

Camarões
ka-ma-royŋsh
shrimps

Canja
kan-zhuh
chicken broth

Caracóis
ka-ra-koysh
snails

Caril
ka-ril
curry

Carne de porco à Alentejana
karn duh por-koo ah a-len-tee-zha-nuh
pork and clams

Carnes
kar-nesh
meat dishes

Carnes frias
kar-nesh free-yuhsh
cold meats

Caseiro
ka-say-roo
homemade

Cenouras
seh-nor-uhsh
carrots

Chanfana da Bairrada
shan-fah-nuh duh by-rah-duh
kid stew

Churrasco
shoo-rash-koo
barbecue

Coelho
koh-el-yoo
rabbit

Coentrada
cwen-tra-duh
with coriander

Com alho
comŋ al-yoo
with garlic

Combinados
com-bee-nah-doosh
snack meals, e.g. burger/chips

Com guarnição *comŋ gwar-nee-<u>ssown</u>*	with garnish
Com natas *comŋ <u>na</u>-tuhsh*	with cream/cream sauce
Costeletas de porco *cosh-tuh-<u>lay</u>-tuhsh duh <u>por</u>-koo*	pork chops
Couvert *coo-<u>ver</u>*	cover charge
Cozido *coh-<u>zee</u>-doo*	boiled/poached
Cozido à Portuguesa *coh-<u>zee</u>-doo ah Por-too-<u>gay</u>-suh*	boiled meat and vegetables
Creme de marisco *crem duh ma-<u>rish</u>-koo*	creamy seafood soup
Croquete de carne *kroh-<u>ket</u> duh <u>karn</u>*	meat croquette
Cru *kroo*	raw
Da época *duh <u>eh</u>-poh-kuh*	of the season
Diversos *dee-<u>ver</u>-soosh*	miscellaneous
Ementa turística *ay-<u>men</u>-tuh too-<u>reesh</u>-tee-kuh*	tourist menu
Empada de galinha *em-<u>pa</u>-duh duh ga-<u>lin</u>-yuh*	small chicken pie
Enguias de caldeirada *en-<u>ghee</u>-uhsh duh cal-day-<u>ra</u>-duh*	eel stew
Ensopado *en-soh-<u>pa</u>-doo*	stew served on bread slices
Entradas *en-<u>trah</u>-duhsh*	starters
Escabeche *shca-<u>besh</u>*	marinated

Escalopes de peru
shca-lopsh duh pe-roo

turkey escalopes

Especialidade da casa
shpeh-see-ah-lee-dah-duh duh kah-suh

house speciality

Estufado
shtoo-fah-doo

braised

Estufado de borrego
shtoo-fah-doo duh boh-ray-goo

lamb stew

Farturas
far-too-ruhsh

long doughnuts

Feijoada Transmontana
fay-zhoh-a-duh trans-mon-ta-nuh

bean/offal stew from Trás-os-Montes

Fígado/iscas
fee-ga-doo/eesh-kuhsh

liver/liver strips

Filetes de pescada
fee-let-esh duh pesh-ka-duh

hake fillets

Flambado
flam-ba-doo

flambé

Folhado de salsicha
fol-ya-doo duh sal-see-shuh

sausage in flaky pastry

Francesinha
fran-seh-seen-yuh

huge, layered hot sandwich

Frango piri-piri
fran-goo pee-ree-pee-ree

roast chicken with piri-piri sauce

Frio
free-oo

cold

Frito
free-too

fried

Frutas
fru-tuhsh

fruit

Frutas da época
fru-tuhsh duh eh-poh-kuh

fruit of the season

Fumado *foo-mah-doo*	smoked
Gambas *gam-buhsh*	prawns
Gelados *zhuh-lah-doosh*	ice cream
Gratinado *gra-tee-na-doo*	au gratin
Grelhado *grel-yah-doo*	grilled
Guarnição *gwar-nee-sown*	garnish
Guisado *ghee-sa-doo*	stewed/braised
IVA incluído *ee-vuh in-cloo-ee-doo*	VAT included
Javali *zha-vuh-lee*	wild boar
Laranja descascada *la-ran-zhuh desh-kash-kah-duh*	peeled orange
Legumes *leh-goomsh*	vegetables
Legumes cozidos *leh-goomsh coh-zee-doosh*	boiled vegetables
Leitão *lay-town*	roast suckling pig
Linguado grelhado *lin-gwa-doo grel-yah-doo*	grilled sole
Lista de vinhos *leesh-tuh duh vin-yoosh*	wine list
Lulas grelhadas *loo-luhsh grel-ya-duhsh*	grilled squid

Maçã assada
mah-ssan a-ssah-duh

baked apple

Mal passado
mal pah-ssah-doo

rare

Marisco
mah-reesh-koo

seafood

Médio
meh-dee-yoo

medium

Melão com presunto
mel-own comn pre-sun-too

melon with ham

Migas
mee-guhsh

fried pork/bread

Mil folhas
mil fol-yuhsh

mille feuille (vanilla slice)

Miolos
mee-oh-loosh

ox brain

Molho
mol-yoo

sauce

Molho branco
mol-yoo bran-koo

white sauce

Mousse de chocolate
mooss duh sho-ko-lat

chocolate mousse

Na brasa
nuh brah-suh

charcoal-grilled

Na chapa
nuh sha-puh

cooked on a hot plate

Na frigideira
nuh free-zhee-day-ruh

pan-cooked

No espeto
noo shpay-too

on the spit

Omeleta (de...)
om-eh-leh-tuh (duh...)

omelette

Ovos...
o-voosh...

...cozidos
coh-zee-doosh

eggs

boiled

...escalfados
shcal-fa-doosh

poached

...estrelados/fritos
shtrel-a-doosh/free-toosh

fried

...mexidos
meh-shee-doosh

scrambled

Ovos doces/doce de ovos
o-voosh doss-esh/doss duh o-voosh

sweet eggs (very sweet mixture)

Panado
pah-na-doo

in breadcrumbs

Panik
pa-nik

pain au chocolat (can also be savoury)

Pão e manteiga
pown eh man-tay-guh

bread and butter

Pastéis de bacalhau
pash-tay-yeesh duh ba-kal-yowu

salted cod/potato cakes

Pastel
pash-tel

salted cod fish

Pastel de nata (de Belém)
pash-tel duh na-tuh (duh beh-laymn)

small custard tart

Pataniscas
pa-ta-nish-kuhsh

cod cake nibbles

Paté de fígado
pa-tay duh fee-ga-doo

liver patê

Peixe
paysh

fish

Picante
pee-kant

spicy

Pratinhos *pra-teen-yoosh*	nibbles/snacks
Prato de buchos *pra-too duh boo-shoosh*	plate of pig's innards in sauce
Prato de moelas *pra-too duh moh-ay-luhsh*	plate of chicken 'bits' in sauce
Prato do dia *pra-too doo dee-yuh*	dish of the day
Prato principal *pra-too prin-see-pal*	main course
Pratos frios/quentes *pra-toosh free-oosh/kent-esh*	cold/hot dishes
Prego no pão *pray-goo noo powŋ*	hot steak sandwich
Pudim flan *pu-deemŋ flan*	crème caramel
Pudim molotov *pu-deemŋ mo-lo-tov*	Molotov pudding (meringue)
Puré *pu-ray*	mashed/puréed
Puré de batatas *pu-ray duh ba-ta-tuhsh*	mashed/puréed potatoes
Queijadas *kay-zha-duhsh*	'cheese' cakes
Queijo da Ilha *kay-zhoo duh il-yuh*	cheese from the Azores
Queijo de Évora *kay-zhoo duh eh-vo-ruh*	Évora cheese
Queijo do Monte *kay-zhoo doo mont*	ewe's cheese
Queijo da Serra *kay-zhoo duh sair-rah*	cheese from the Serra mountains

Queijos *kay-zhoosh*	cheese selection
Quente *kent*	hot
Recheado *reh-shee-a-doo*	stuffed/filled
Rissóis *ree-ssoysh*	deep-fried rissoles
Rissol de camarão *ree-ssol duh ka-ma-rown*	shrimp rissole
Rojões *ro-zhoynsh*	pork pieces fried in fat
Salada de fruta *sa-lah-duh duh fru-tuh*	fruit salad
Salada mista *sa-lah-duh mish-tuh*	mixed salad (tomato/onion)
Saladas *sa-lah-duhsh*	salads
Salgados *sal-ga-doosh*	savoury nibbles
Salteado *sal-tee-a-doo*	sautéed
Sardinhas assadas/grelhadas *sar-din-yuhsh a-ssa-duhsh/grel-ya-duhsh*	grilled sardines
Serviço incluído *ser-vee-ssoo in-cloo-ee-doo*	service included
Sobremesas/doces *sob-ray-may-suhsh/doss-esh*	desserts
Sopa de feijão *soh-puh duh fay-zhown*	bean soup
Sopa de legumes *soh-puh duh leh-goomsh*	vegetable soup

Sopas	soups
soh-puhsh	
Tarte de amêndoa	almond tart
tart duh a-men-doh-uh	
Temperado	spiced/flavoured
tem-per-ra-doo	
Torta de laranja	orange roulade
tor-tuh duh la-ran-zhuh	
Tripas à moda do Minho	tripe Minho-style
tree-puhsh ah mo-duh doo meen-yoo	
Truta recheada	trout filled with ham
tru-tuh re-shee-a-duh	
Vitela no espeto	spit-roast veal
vee-teh-luh noo shpay-too	

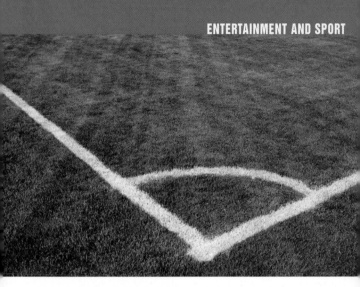

ENTERTAINMENT AND SPORT

The cinema is very cheap in Portugal, and is once more rising in popularity. Most towns have a small cinema, with multiscreen complexes in Lisbon, at the Amoreiras shopping centre, and elsewhere, often showing films until quite late at night. Lisbon and Porto host annual film festivals. Foreign films are usually subtitled (*com legendas*).

Theatre, opera, concerts and art exhibitions are all popular, especially in Lisbon and Porto, where there are a number of places to be entertained. Tickets for events can be bought at the box office, at ticket sales kiosks and at some tourist offices. Discos and nightclubs are abundant in the larger cities and the Algarve. Most open from about 10pm onwards, some staying open until 5/6am. Entrance prices vary considerably, and often the entry ticket allows you a free drink once inside. Be cautious about 'free tab' tickets, where you mark on your ticket what you drink all night – the final bill may well catch you out. Drinks inside clubs can be very expensive, unless you go to a smaller club outside the large towns.

Fado music is the national sound and can be heard in Fado houses or restaurants in Lisbon (Bairro Alto and Alfama in particular), Coimbra (which has its own type), and around the country. When the singer is about to start, the lights are dimmed and you are expected to stop eating and listen in silence.

Bullfights are not as popular as in Spain, but there are various bullrings throughout Portugal, the largest being in Lagos and the Campo Pequeno ring in Lisbon. Portuguese bullfights are different from their Spanish counterparts; there is a lot more horsemanship and displays of 'bravery' from groups of men trying to leap onto the bull's back. However, although the bull might not be killed in the ring itself, it will invariably be killed afterwards.

Football matches, on every level, are fanatically supported, with matches often taking place on a Sunday afternoon. Tickets can be bought direct from the ground on the day, although important fixtures, such as Benfica, FC Porto and Sporting Lisbon sell out quickly.

Museums, exhibitions and art displays are abundant, and most offer discount rates to students, children and OAPs; the normal cost is not generally very expensive. Most close on Mondays – check with the tourist offices for details.

There is no network of public leisure centres as you might be used to in the UK, although many towns have municipal swimming pools. You are usually required to wear a bathing hat to swim. There are also private gyms, and hotel-run health centres, especially in the Algarve, many with tennis courts as well as indoor facilities.

Outdoor pursuits are popular, especially those connected with the sea, such as surfing, windsailing and fishing. Most are available in Algarve resorts and around the Lisbon coastline.

Cinema	O cinema *oo see-<u>nay</u>-muh*
Theatre	O teatro *oo tee-<u>a</u>-troo*
Nightclub	A boîte *uh bwat*
Disco	A discoteca *uh dish-koh-<u>teh</u>-kuh*
Dance hall	A sala de festas *uh <u>sa</u>-luh duh <u>fesh</u>-tuhsh*
Social club	O grêmio *oo <u>greh</u>-mee-yoo*
Museum	O museu *oo moo-<u>say</u>-oo*
Party/Celebration	A festa *uh <u>fesh</u>-tuh*
Fado music bar	A casa de Fado *uh <u>ka</u>-suh duh <u>fah</u>-doo*
Gallery	A galeria *uh ga-ler-<u>ree</u>-yuh*
Exhibition hall/Gallery	A sala de exposições *uh <u>sa</u>-luh duh shpo-see-<u>soynsh</u>*
Ballet	O balé *oo ba-<u>leh</u>*
Opera	A ópera *uh <u>o</u>-peh-ruh*
Review (theatre)	A revista *uh reh-<u>vish</u>-tuh*
Bullfight	A tourada *uh toh-<u>ra</u>-duh*
Event	O espectáculo *oo shpe-<u>ta</u>-ku-loo*
Circus	O circo *oo <u>seer</u>-koo*

BUYING A TICKET

One ticket, please
Uma entrada/Um bilhete, por favor
oo-muh en-<u>tra</u>-duh/oomη bil-<u>yet</u>, por fa-<u>vor</u>

A child's ticket
Um bilhete de criança
oomη bil-<u>yet</u> duh cree-<u>ya</u>η-ssuh

I'd like to reserve 3 tickets
Queria reservar 3 bilhetes
<u>kree</u>-uh re-ser-<u>var</u> traysh bil-<u>yet</u>-esh

How much is it?
Quanto é?
<u>kwan</u>-too eh?

Do you have tickets for the 7 o'clock performance?
Há bilhetes para as sete?
Ah bil-<u>yet</u>-esh <u>puh</u>-ruh azh set?

Is there a discount...?
Fazem desconto...?
<u>fa</u>-zaymη desh-<u>con</u>-too...?

...today
...hoje
...ozh

...for students
...para estudantes
...<u>puh</u>-ruh shtoo-<u>dan</u>-tush

...for children
...para crianças
...<u>puh</u>-ruh cree-<u>ya</u>η-suhsh

...for pensioners
...para os idosos
...<u>puh</u>-ruh oosh ee-<u>doh</u>-soosh

...for groups
...para grupos
...<u>puh</u>-ruh <u>gru</u>-poosh

When does...open?
A que horas abre...?
uh kay <u>or</u>-uhsh <u>a</u>-bray...?

When does...close?
A que horas fecha...?
uh kay <u>or</u>-uhsh <u>fay</u>-shuh...?

When does...start?
A que horas começa...?
uh kay <u>or</u>-uhsh coh-<u>may</u>-ssuh...?

When does...finish?
A que horas termina...?
uh kay <u>or</u>-uhsh ter-<u>mee</u>-nuh...?

...the film	...o filme *...oo film*
...the play	...a peça *...uh <u>pay</u>-ssuh*
...the concert	...o concerto *...oo con-<u>ser</u>-too*
...the opera	...a ópera *...uh <u>o</u>-peh-ruh*
...the (afternoon) showing	...a sessão (da tarde)/a matinée *...uh se-<u>ssown</u> (duh tard)/uh ma-tee-<u>nay</u>*
...the (evening) performance	...a sessão (da noite) *...uh se-<u>ssown</u> (duh noyt)*
I'd like...	Queria... *<u>kree</u>-uh...*
...stalls (orchestra)	...platéia *...pla-<u>tay</u>-uh*
...circle (mezzanine)	...balcão *...bal-<u>kown</u>*
...aisle	...coxia *...co-<u>shee</u>-uh*
...a (10) euro ticket	um bilhete de (10) euros *oomn bil-<u>yet</u> duh (desh) <u>air</u>-roosh*
Are they numbered?	Os lugares têm números? *oosh loo-<u>gar</u>-esh <u>tay</u>-emn <u>nu</u>-meh-roosh?*
At the front/back	À frente/atrás *ah frent/uh-<u>trash</u>*
In the middle	No meio *noo <u>may</u>-oo*
A programme	Um programa *oomn pro-<u>gra</u>-muh*

Is there an interval?	Tem intervalo? *taymη in-ter-va-loo?*
How long is it?	Quanto tempo dura? *kwan-too tem-poo du-ruh?*
Is there a bar?	Há um bar? *Ah oomη bar?*
Where is the cloakroom?	Onde é o vestiário? *ond eh oo vesh-tee-ah-ree-yoo?*
Where are the toilets?	Onde são os lavabos? *ond sown oosh la-vah-boosh?*

AT THE DISCO/NIGHTCLUB

How much is the entry price?	Quanto é para entrar? *kwan-too eh puh-ruh en-trar?*
Does it include a drink?	O preço inclui uma bebida? *oo pray-ssoo in-cloo-ee oo-muh beh-bee-duh?*
What type of music is it?	Que tipo de música há? *kuh ti-poo duh moo-see-kuh ah?*
Is there live music?	Há música ao vivo? *ah moo-see-kuh ow vee-voo?*

AT A BULLFIGHT

Where is the bullring?	Onde fica a praça de touros? *ond fee-kuh uh pra-ssuh duh toh-roosh?*
When is there a bullfight?	Quando há uma corrida? *kwan-doo ah oo-muh coh-ree-duh?*
How long does it last?	Quanto tempo dura? *kwan-too tem-poo du-ruh?*

A ticket…	Uma entrada… *oo-muh en-<u>tra</u>-duh…*
…in the shade	…à sombra *…ah <u>som</u>-bruh*
…in the sun	…ao sol *…ow sol*
…in a good place	…num lugar bom *…noom loo-<u>gar</u> bomη*
Do you hire cushions?	Aluga almofadas? *a-<u>loo</u>-guh al-mo-<u>fa</u>-duhsh?*
Are there refreshments?	Há bebidas? *ah beh-<u>bee</u>-duhsh?*

You may hear:

Já não há entradas/bilhetes *zha nowη ah en-<u>tra</u>-duhsh/bil-<u>yet</u>-esh*	There are no tickets left
É gratis *eh <u>grá</u>-tish*	It's free
Não fazemos reservas *nowη fa-<u>zay</u>-moosh re-<u>ser</u>-vuhsh*	We don't take reservations
Não há venda com antecedência *nowη ah <u>ven</u>-duh comη an-teh-se-<u>den</u>-see-yuh*	There are no advance sales
A entrada é gratuita para menores de…anos *uh en-<u>tra</u>-duh eh gra-too-<u>ee</u>-tuh <u>puh</u>-ruh meh-<u>nor</u>-esh duh…<u>a</u>-noosh*	Free entry to under…'s
O filme tem legendas *oo film taymη leh-<u>zhen</u>-duhsh*	The film has subtitles

SPORT

What time is the match?	A que horas é a partida/o jogo? *uh kay <u>or</u>-uhsh eh uh par-<u>tee</u>-duh/oo <u>zho</u>-goo?*
A ticket...	Um bilhete... *oomη bil-<u>yet</u>...*
...in the stand	...na tribuna *...nuh tree-<u>bu</u>-nuh*
...on the terrace	...na geral *...nuh zheh-<u>ral</u>*
Who's playing this week?	Quem joga esta semana? *kaymη <u>zho</u>-guh <u>eh</u>-shtuh suh-<u>mah</u>-nuh?*
Can one...here?	Pode-se...aqui? *<u>pod</u>-suh...a-<u>key</u>?*
...swim	...nadar *...na-<u>dar</u>*
...dive	...mergulhar *...mer-gul-<u>yar</u>*
...fish	...pescar *...pesh-<u>kar</u>*
...go sailing	...fazer vela *...fa-<u>zair</u> <u>veh</u>-luh*
...water-ski	...fazer esqui aquático *...fa-<u>zair</u> shkey a-<u>kwa</u>-tee-koo*
...windsurf	...fazer windsurf *...fa-<u>zair</u> windsurf*
...hire pedalos	...alugar gaivotas *...a-loo-<u>gar</u> guy-<u>voh</u>-tuhsh*
...do water sports	...fazer desportos aquáticos *...fa-<u>zair</u> desh-<u>por</u>-toosh a-<u>kwa</u>-tee-koosh*
...go horse riding	...andar a cavalo *...an-<u>dar</u> uh ka-<u>va</u>-loo*

...play tennis	...jogar ténis ..._zho-gar te_-nish
...hunt	...caçar ..._ka-ssar_
Is there a...here/near here?	Há...aqui/perto daqui? _ah...a-key/per-too duh-key?_
...a golf course	...um campo de golfe ..._oomη cam_-poo duh golf
...an (indoor) swimming pool	...uma piscina (coberta) ..._oo-muh pee-ssee_-nuh (ko-_ber_-tuh)
...a sports centre	...um centro desportivo ..._oomη sen_-troo desh-por-_tee_-voo
...a tennis court	...um campo de ténis ..._oomη cam_-poo duh te-nish
...a gym/healthclub	...um ginásio ..._oomη zhi-na_-see-yoo
...a horse-riding centre	...um centro hípico ..._oomη sen_-troo ee-pee-koo
Can I hire...?	Posso alugar...? _poh_-ssoo a-loo-_gar_...?
...a bicycle	...uma bicicleta ..._oo_-muh bee-see-_klay_-tuh
...a (small) boat	...um barco (pequeno) ..._oomη bar_-koo (pe-_kay_-noo)
...fishing equipment	...equipamento de pesca ..._eh-kee-pa-men_-too duh _pesh_-kuh
...water skis	...esquis aquáticos ..._shkeysh a-kwa_-tee-koosh
...a surfboard	...uma prancha de surf ..._oo_-muh _pran_-shuh duh surf
...a tennis racket	...uma raqueta de ténis ..._oo_-muh ra-_ke_-tuh duh _te_-nish

...equipment for...	...equipamento para... ...*eh-kee-pa-men-too puh-ruh*...
Do you have to pay to get in?	Tem que pagar para entrar? *taymŋ kuh puh-gar puh-ruh en-trar?*
Do you have to be a member?	Tem que ser sócio? *taymŋ kuh sair soh-see-yoo?*
How much is it per hour/day?	Quanto é por hora/por dia? *kwan-too eh por or-uh/por dee-yuh?*
Where are the changing rooms?	Onde são os vestiários? *ond sowŋ oosh vesh-tee-ar-ree-yoosh?*
Do you have a locker key?	Tem chave para o cacifo? *taymŋ shav puh-ruh oo ka-see-foo?*
I would like...lessons	Queria ter lições de... *kree-uh tair lee-soyŋsh duh...*
Is there a lifeguard?	Há salva-vidas? *ah sal-vuh-vee-duhsh?*

You may hear:

Tem que/de ser sócio *taymŋ kuh/duh sair soh-see-yoo*	You have to be a member
Tem touca? *taymŋ toh-kuh?*	Do you have a swimming cap?
Faça favor de preencher esta ficha *fa-ssuh fa-vor duh pray-en-shair eh-shtuh fee-shuh*	Please fill in this form
Tem que pagar depósito de (5) euros *taymŋ kuh puh-gar duh-poh-see- too duh (sin-koo) air-roosh*	You have to pay a deposit of (5) euros
Tem de tomar duche antes de entrar *taymŋ duh toh-mar doosh an-tush duh en-trar*	You have to shower before going in

HEALTH

You can obtain free emergency treatment in Portugal on production of the E111 form, available from UK post offices. You may be asked to pay for some treatments, but you can claim the money back (with a receipt) once you return home. Consultations with a GP are charged for, as are dental visits, which are extremely expensive.

In case of an emergency, seek the local casualty department at the hospital (*Emergências*); in non-urgent cases you can visit the local health centre (*Centro de Saúde*), or doctor's surgery (*Consultório*).

The emergency telephone number 112 will get you through to the three services: fire (*Bombeiros*), ambulance (*Ambulância*) or police (*Polícia*). It is operated in Portuguese, French and English.

Many people use the chemist (*a farmácia*) as the first stop for (free) medical advice on non-serious complaints. Chemists are very efficient and can usually sort out minor ailments quickly and for less money. A list of stand-by chemists open out of hours (*Farmácia de Serviço*) is displayed in the chemist's shop window and is published in the local paper.

ASKING FOR HELP

Could you help me, please?	Podia ajudar-me, por favor? *po-dee-yuh a-zhoo-dar-muh, por fa-vor?*
I don't speak Portuguese	Não falo português *nowη fa-loo por-too-gaysh*
Do you speak English?	Fala inglês? *fa-luh in-glaysh?*
I'm not well	Não estou bem *nowη shtoh baymη*
I need...	Preciso... *pruh-see-soo...*
...a doctor	...dum médico *...doom meh-dee-koo*
...an interpreter	...dum intérprete *...doom in-ter-pret*
...to go to hospital	...de ir ao hospital *...duh eer ow osh-pee-tal*
Where is...?	Onde é...? *ond eh...?*
...the hospital	...o hospital *...oo osh-pee-tal*
...the doctor's surgery	...o consultório médico *...oo con-sul-toh-ree-yoo meh-dee-koo*

...the casualty/A&E entrance	...a entrada para emergências *...uh en-<u>tra</u>-duh <u>puh</u>-ruh eh-mer-<u>zhen</u>-see-yuhsh*
It's urgent/serious	É urgente/grave *eh ur-<u>zhent</u>/grav*
I am ill/injured	Estou doente/ferido/a *shtoh doh-<u>ent</u>/feh-<u>ree</u>-doo/uh*
I've had an accident	Tive um acidente *teev oomη a-ssee-<u>dent</u>*
Can you call an ambulance?	Pode chamar uma ambulância? *pod sha-<u>mar</u> <u>oo</u>-muh am-boo-<u>lan</u>-see-yuh?*
Could you take me to hospital?	Podia levar-me ao hospital? *po-<u>dee</u>-yuh luh-<u>var</u>-muh ow osh-pee-<u>tal</u>?*
Is there a doctor...?	Há um médico...? *ah oomη <u>meh</u>-dee-koo...?*
...here	...aqui *...a-<u>key</u>*
...in the hotel	...no hotel *...noo o-<u>tel</u>*
...in the campsite	...no parque (de campismo) *...noo park (duh cam-<u>pizh</u>-moo)*
Is there a nurse/a first aid box?	Há um/a enfermeiro/a/caixa de primeiros-socorros? *ah oomη/<u>oo</u>-muh en-fer-<u>may</u>-roo/en-fer-<u>may</u>-ruh/<u>kye</u>-shuh duh pree-<u>may</u>-roosh-soh-<u>koh</u>-roosh?*
Can the doctor come...?	O médico pode vir...? *oo <u>meh</u>-dee-koo pod veer...?*
...now	...agora *...a-<u>goh</u>-ruh*
...today	...hoje *...ozh*

...as soon as possible	...logo que possível ..._loh_-goo kuh poh-_ssee_-vel
My address is...	A minha morada é... uh _meen_-yuh mo-_ra_-duh eh...
I'm at the (Sol) hotel	Estou no hotel (Sol) shtoh noo o-_tel_ (Sol)
We are in the market	Estamos ao mercado _shta_-moosh ow mer-_ka_-doo

AT THE DOCTOR'S

What time is the surgery open?	A que horas abre o consultório? uh kay _or_-uhsh _a_-bray oo con-sul-_toh_-ree-yoo?
Could you give me an appointment with...?	Podia dar-me uma consulta com...? po-_dee_-yuh _dar_-muh _oo_-muh con-_sul_-tuh comη...?
...the doctor (GP)	...o/a médico/a ...oo/uh _meh_-dee-koo/uh
...the eye specialist	...o/a oftalmogista ...oo/uh off-tal-moh-_zheess_-tuh
...the gynaecologist	...o/a ginecologista ...oo/uh zhin-ee-ko-lo-_zhiss_-tuh
...the dentist	...o/a dentista ...oo/uh den-_tish_-tuh
...the specialist	...o/a especialista ...oo/uh shpe-see-a-_lish_-tuh
It hurts me here	Dói-me aqui _doy_-muh a-_key_
My...hurts	Dói-me... _doy_-muh...
...ankle	...o tornozelo ...oo tor-noh-_zay_-loo

...arm	...o braço
	...oo <u>brah</u>-ssoo
...breast/chest	...o peito
	...oo <u>pay</u>-too
...ear (inner)	...o ouvido
	...oo oo-<u>vee</u>-doo
...eye	...o olho
	...oo <u>ol</u>-yoo
...finger	...o dedo
	...oo <u>deh</u>-doo
...foot	...o pé
	...oo pay
...hand	...a mão
	...uh mownη
...head	...a cabeça
	...uh ka-<u>bay</u>-suh
...knee	...o joelho
	...oo zhoh-<u>el</u>-yoo
...leg	...a perna
	...uh <u>per</u>-nuh
...lung	...o pulmão
	...oo pul-<u>mownη</u>
...mouth	...a boca
	...uh <u>boh</u>-kuh
...neck	...o pescoço
	...oo pess-<u>koh</u>-ssoo
...nose	...o nariz
	...oo na-<u>reezh</u>
...penis	...o pénis
	...oo <u>peh</u>-nish
...shoulder	...o ombro
	...oo <u>om</u>-broo

...stomach	...o estômago
	...oo _shtoh_-muh-goo
...throat	...a garganta
	...uh gar-_gan_-tuh
...vagina	...a vagina
	...uh va-_zhee_-nuh
...wrist	...o pulso
	...oo _pul_-soo
...elbow	...o cotovelo
	...oo coh-toh-_veh_-loo
...heel	...o calcanhar
	...oo kal-kun-_yar_
...belly/gut	...o ventre/a barriga
	...oo _ven_-truh/uh bah-_ree_-guh
My...hurt	Doem-me...
	doh-emη-muh...
...back (plural in Portuguese)	...as costas
	...uhsh _cosh_-tuhsh
...joints	...as articulações
	...uhsh ar-ti-ku-la-_ssoyη_sh
...eyes	...os olhos
	...oosh _ol_-yoosh
...elbows	...os cotovelos
	...oosh coh-toh-_veh_-loosh
...teeth	...os dentes
	...oosh _den_-tesh
...toes	...os dedos do pé
	...oosh _deh_-doosh doo pay
It hurts...	Dói...
	doy...
...a lot	...muito
	..._mweeη_-too
...a little	...um pouco
	...oomη _poh_-koo

...all the time	...continuamente
	..._con-tin-oo-a-<u>ment</u>_
...sometimes	...de vez em quando
	..._duh vezh aymη <u>kwan</u>-doo_
It's been hurting...	Dói-me...
	<u>doy</u>-muh...
...since yesterday	...desde ontem
	..._<u>desh</u>-duh <u>on</u>-taymη_
...for two days	...há dois dias
	..._ah doysh <u>dee</u>-yuhsh_
...for a few hours	...há umas horas
	..._ah <u>oo</u>-muhsh <u>or</u>-uhsh_
It's a sharp pain	É uma dor aguda
	eh <u>oo</u>-muh dor a-<u>goo</u>-duh
I feel...	Sinto-me...
	<u>sin</u>-too-muh...
...sick	...mal
	..._mal_
...weak	...fraco/a
	..._<u>fra</u>-koo/uh_
...worse	...pior
	..._pee-<u>yor</u>_
...dizzy	...tonto/a
	..._<u>ton</u>-too/uh_
I have a cold	Estou constipado/a
	shtoh con-shti-<u>pa</u>-doo/uh
I am constipated	Tenho prisão do ventre
	<u>tayn</u>-yoo pri-<u>sown</u>η doo <u>ven</u>-truh
I have...	Tenho...
	<u>tayn</u>-yoo...
...cramps	...cãibra
	..._<u>kighη</u>-bruh_

...diarrhoea	...diarreia
	...dee-a-_ray_-uh
...insomnia	...insônia
	...in-_so_-nee-yuh
...a migraine	...uma enxaqueca
	..._oo_-muh en-sha-_keh_-kuh
...a rash	...uma irritação na pele
	..._oo_-muh ee-ree-tuh-_sowη_ nuh pel
...a stiff neck	...torcicolo
	...tor-see-_koh_-loo
...shivers	...arrepios
	...a-reh-_pee_-yoosh
I think I have...	Acho que tenho...
	_ah_-shoo kuh _tayη_-yoo...
...the flu	...a gripe
	...uh greep
...food poisoning	...intoxicação de alimentos
	...in-tox-ee-ka-_sowη_ duh a-lee-_men_-toosh
...indigestion	...indigestão
	...in-dee-zhes-_towη_
...an infection	...uma infecção
	..._oo_-muh in-fek-_sowη_
...sinusitis	...sinusite
	...seen-oo-_seet_
...sun stroke	...insolação
	...in-soh-la-_sowη_
...a temperature	...febre
	..._feh_-breh
It itches	Irrita
	ee-_ree_-tuh

I can't breathe properly/ move (my arm)/walk/sleep	Não consigo respirar bem/mexer (o braço)/andar/dormir *nown con-<u>see</u>-goo resh-pee-<u>rar</u> baymη/meh-<u>shair</u> (oo <u>brah</u>-ssoo)/an-<u>dar</u>/dor-<u>meer</u>*
It's infected/swollen	Está infectado/inchado *shta in-fek-<u>ta</u>-doo/in-<u>sha</u>-doo*
I've lost my appetite	Perdi completamente o apetite *per-<u>dee</u> com-pleh-ta-<u>ment</u> oo a-puh-<u>teet</u>*
What's happened?	O que aconteceu? *oo kuh a-con-tuh-<u>say</u>-oo?*
I've twisted...	Torci... *tor-<u>see</u>...*
I've fallen over	Caí *kigh-<u>yee</u>*
I've burned myself	Quemei-me *kay-<u>may</u>-muh*
I've cut myself	Cortei-me *cor-<u>tay</u>-muh*
I've bumped myself	Magoei-me/Dei uma pancada *ma-go-<u>ay</u>-muh/day <u>oo</u>-muh pan-<u>ka</u>-duh*
I've taken this	Tomei isto *toh-<u>may</u> <u>eesh</u>-too*
My friend/husband/son...	O meu amigo/marido/filho... *oo <u>may</u>-oo a-<u>mee</u>-goo/mah-<u>ree</u>-doo/<u>feel</u>-yoo...*
...is injured	...está ferido *...shta feh-<u>ree</u>-doo*
...is ill	...está doente *...shta doh-<u>ent</u>*
...is unconscious	...está sem sentidos *...shta saymη sen-<u>tee</u>-doosh*

...has fainted	...desmaiou ...*desh-my-oh*
...has had a (heart) attack	...teve um ataque cardíaco ...*tev oomη a-tak kar-dee-a-koo*
...has cut his/her (hand)	...cortou (a mão) ...*kor-toh (uh mowη)*
I've been stung/bitten by...	Fui picado/a/mordido/a por... *fwee pi-ka-doo/uh/mor-dee- doo/uh por...*
...something	...alguma coisa ...*al-goo-muh coy-suh*
...an insect	...um insecto ...*oomη in-seh-too*
...a mosquito	...um mosquito ...*oomη mosh-key-too*
...a wasp/bee	...uma vespa/abelha ...*oo-muh vesh-puh/a-bel-yuh*
...a snake	...uma cobra ...*oo-muh coh-bruh*
...a dog	...um cão ...*oomη cowη*
...a jellyfish	...uma alforreca ...*oo-muh al-foh-reh-kuh*

GENERAL CONDITIONS

I have/s/he has...	Tenho/tem... *tayn-yoo/taymη...*
...asthma	...asma ...*azh-muh*
...diabetes	...diabetes ...*dee-a-beh-tesh*
...high/low blood pressure	...tensão arterial alta/baixa ...*ten-sowη ar-teh-ree-yal al- tuh/bye-shuh*

I'm allergic to penicillin/antibiotics	Sou alérgico/a a penicilina/antibiótico *soh a-<u>ler</u>-zhee-koo/uh uh pe-nee-see-<u>lee</u>-nuh/an-tee-bee-<u>o</u>-tee-koo*
I take the pill/this medication	Tomo a pílula/este medicamento *<u>toh</u>-moo uh <u>pi</u>-loo-luh/esht meh-dee-ka-<u>men</u>-too*
I'm (3 months) pregnant	Estou grávida (de três meses) *shtoh <u>gra</u>-vee-duh (duh traysh <u>may</u>-zesh)*
I have a heart condition	Sofro do coração *<u>soh</u>-froo doo koh-ruh-<u>sown</u>*
I had a heart attack	Tive um ataque cardíaco *teev umη a-<u>tak</u> kar-<u>dee</u>-a-koo*

QUESTIONS

Could you give me something...?	Podia dar-me alguma coisa...? *po-<u>dee</u>-yuh <u>dar</u>-muh al-<u>goo</u>-muh <u>coy</u>-suh...?*
...for the pain	...para a dor *...<u>puh</u>-ruh uh dor*
...to sleep	...para dormir *...<u>puh</u>-ruh dor-<u>meer</u>*
I (don't) want...	(não) Quero... *(nowη) <u>kair</u>-roo...*
...injections	...injecções *...in-zhek-<u>soyη</u>sh*
...suppositories	...supositórios *...su-poh-see-<u>toh</u>-ree-yoosh*
When do I have to take the medicine?	Quando tenho que tomar a medicina? *<u>kwan</u>-doo <u>tayη</u>-yoo kuh toh-<u>mar</u> uh meh-dee-<u>see</u>-nuh?*

How often do I take it each day?	Quantas vezes tomo por dia? *kwan-tuhsh vay-zesh toh-moo por dee-yuh?*
Do I have to stay in bed?	Tenho que ficar de cama? *tayn-yoo kuh fee-kar duh kah-muh?*
Can I drive?	Posso conduzir? *poh-ssoo con-doo-zeer?*
Is it okay to go swimming?	Posso ir nadar? *poh-ssoo eer na-dar?*
Is it catching?	É contagioso? *eh con-ta-zhee-oh-soo?*

AT THE OPTICIAN'S

Could you repair my glasses?	Podia consertar os meus óculos? *po-dee-yuh con-ser-tar oosh may-oosh o-koo-loosh?*
I've lost my contact lenses	Perdi as lentes *per-dee uhsh len-tesh*
I have something in this eye	Tenho alguma coisa neste olho *tayn-yoo al-goo-muh coy-suh nesht ol-yoo*
I need some cleaning fluid	Preciso de líquido de limpeza *pruh-see-soo duh li-kee-doo duh lim-pay-zuh*

AT THE DENTIST'S

It aches here	Dói aqui *doy a-key*
This tooth/molar/my gum hurts	Dói-me este dente/molar/a gengiva *doy-muh esht dent/moh-lar/uh zhen-zhee-vuh*

A filling has fallen out	Caiu-me um chumbo
	kigh-yoo-muh oomη shum-boo
I have an abscess	Tenho um abcesso
	tayn-yoo oomη ab-sess-oo
Please don't take out my tooth	Por favor não arranque o dente
	por fa-vor nowη a-rank oo dent
Could you fix my dentures?	Podia arranjar a dentadura?
	po-dee-yuh a-ran-zhar uh den-ta-doo-ruh?
I'm scared of injections	Tenho medo de injecções
	tayn-yoo meh-doo duh in-zhek-soyηsh
I'm very nervous	Estou muito nervoso/a
	shtoh mweeη-too ner-voh-soo/uh
I'm pregnant	Estou grávida
	shtoh gra-vee-duh

PAYING

How much do I owe you?	Quanto lhe devo?
	kwan-too lyuh day-voo?
Do I have to pay something now?	Tenho que pagar alguma coisa agora?
	tayn-yoo kuh puh-gar al-goo-muh coy-suh a-goh-ruh?
I have this insurance	Tenho este seguro
	tayn-yoo esht se-goo-roo
Could you...?	Podia...?
	po-dee-yuh...?
...give me a receipt	...dar-me um recibo
	...dar-muh oomη re-see-boo
...give me a medical certificate	...dar-me um certificado
	...dar-muh oomη ser-tee-fee-ka-doo

...fill this in for me

...preencher isto para mim
...*pray-en-shair eesh-too puh-ruh meemη*

Do I need to come back?

Preciso de voltar?
pruh-see-soo duh vol-tar?

When?

Quando?
kwan-doo?

You may hear:

Onde dói?
ond doy?

Where does it hurt?

Tome isto
tom eesh-too

Take this

Cada (duas) horas
cah-duh (doo-uhsh) or-uhsh

Every (two) hours

Antes/Depois da comida
an-tesh/de-poysh duh co-mee-duh

Before/After food

(quatro) Vezes por dia
(kwa-troo) vay-zesh por dee-yuh

(four) Times a day

Fique de cama
feek duh kah-muh

Stay in bed

Não tome banho
nowη tom ban-yoo

Don't bathe

Tem que ir ao hospital
taymη kuh eer ow osh-pee-tal

You have to go to the hospital

Volte amanhã
volt uh-mun-yaη

Come back tomorrow

See also page 148 for the pharmacist.

SPECIAL NEEDS

Portugal, in general, is not very well geared up for people with special needs. There are a few toilets for the disabled and some parking spaces but, on the whole, this is an area still lacking throughout. Some of the modern buses now have lowering steps for wheelchairs and priority seating for the disabled, as do some trains.

Few taxis are able to accommodate wheelchairs, although there is a service available in Lisbon, and a special dial-a-ride bus service in Lisbon and Porto.

Is there a lift?	Há elevador?
	ah uh-leh-vuh-<u>dor</u>?
I/s/he can't walk far	Não posso/pode andar muito
	nowη <u>poh</u>-ssoo/pod an-<u>dar</u> <u>mween</u>-too
Are there toilets for the disabled?	Há sanitários para deficientes?
	ah sa-nee-<u>ta</u>-ree-oosh <u>puh</u>-ruh deh-fee-see-<u>ent</u>-esh?
Is there wheelchair access?	Há acesso para cadeiras de rodas?
	Ah a-<u>seh</u>-ssoo <u>puh</u>-ruh ka-<u>day</u>-ruhsh duh <u>roh</u>-duhsh?
Will a wheelchair fit?	Cabe uma cadeira de rodas?
	cab <u>oo</u>-muh ka-<u>day</u>-ruh duh <u>roh</u>-duhsh?
Do you have facilities for the disabled?	Tem instalações para os deficientes?
	taymη in-sta-la-<u>soyη</u>sh <u>puh</u>-ruh oosh deh-fee-see-<u>ent</u>-esh?
Do you have a room on the ground-floor?	Tem um quarto no rés-do-chão?
	taymη oomη <u>kwar</u>-too noo resh-doo-<u>showη</u>?

SHOPPING AND SERVICES

Most shops open from 8.30/9am until 1pm, then close for lunch until about 3/4pm. They then reopen until early evening (7/7.30pm). They close on Saturday afternoons and all day on Sundays, apart from some shops (mainly food stores) in the tourist areas.

Large shopping centres, with a variety of shop units, open all day, and many until quite late at night during the week and weekends. However, despite the presence of the large shopping stores, many Portuguese shoppers still prefer to do their shopping daily from small retail businesses selling fresh produce.

Markets are alive from early morning, but often start packing up mid-afternoon, so you have to be there promptly to buy your fresh bread and fish.

Feiras, or travelling markets, visit towns once a month or fortnight. Here you can buy all manner of objects, from plastic washing-up bowls, to bargain clothes and shoes, to handmade articles.

August can be a tricky month for visiting small shops and bars, as this is the month when people generally shut for the summer holidays. Bear this in mind when planning your visits, especially in quiet, rural areas.

SUPERMARKETS AND HYPERMARKETS

There are an increasing number of larger shopping complexes, mostly on the outskirts of major towns but with some in city centres. They sell a huge range of products, including food, clothing, household items, books, music and domestic appliances. Many have shop units in the entrance, as well as eating places, and some have cinemas, so you can spend your whole leisure time there if you so wish. They are popular meeting places for young people.

Shopping trolleys operate in the same way as in the UK, needing a coin to release them.

You may be required to leave your bag in a special bag-deposit section at the entrance of some supermarkets, for security reasons. You will be given a ticket or token to reclaim it later.

In the fruit and vegetables section, you may have to weigh your own food on an electronic machine – these often require you to push the correct button with the name of the item on it, so you need to know the names of the items you are weighing.

There is usually a delicatessen counter, and fish/meat sections, where you take a ticket and wait for your number to be called.

For numbers see page 183.

You may see:

Autoserviço	Self-service
Caixa	Check out/Till

Desconto	Discount
Elevador	Lift
Entrada	Entrance
Escada rolante	Escalator
Escadas	Stairs
Esgotado	Sold out
Liquidação total	Total liquidation (everything must go)
Oferta (especial)	Offer (special)
Pague 1, leve 2!	Buy one, get one free!
Pechincha	Bargain
Piso/Andar	Floor
Preço (reduzido)	Price (reduced)
Pré-pagamento	Prepayment
Reduções	Reductions
Saída	Exit
Saldos/Baixa de preços	Department/Section
Secção	Sales
Segunda mão	Second-hand
Usado/a	Used

SHOPS

Department store/warehouse	Armazém *ar-ma-__zaymn__*
Toy shop	Casa/Loja de brinquedos *__ka__-suh/__lo__-zhuh duh brin-__kay__-doosh*
Furniture shop	Casa/Loja de móveis *__ka__-suh/__lo__-zhuh duh __moh__-vay-ish*
Shopping centre	Centro comercial *__sen__-troo coh-mer-see-__yal__*

Clothing	Confecções/roupa *con-fek-<u>soynsh</u>/<u>roh</u>-puh*
Music/Record shop	Discoteca/loja de música *dish-koh-<u>teh</u>-kuh/<u>lo</u>-zhuh duh <u>moo</u>-see-kuh*
Drugstore/household goods	Drogaria *droh-guh-<u>ree</u>-yuh*
Chemist	Farmácia *far-<u>mass</u>-see-yuh*
Florist	Florista *floh-<u>rish</u>-tuh*
Fruitshop	Frutaria *froo-tuh-<u>ree</u>-yuh*
Hypermarket	Hipermercado *ee-per-mer-<u>ka</u>-doo*
Dairy	Leitaria *lay-tuh-<u>ree</u>-yuh*
Bookshop	Livraria *lee-vruh-<u>ree</u>-yuh*
Sports shop	Loja de desporto *<u>lo</u>-zhuh duh desh-<u>por</u>-too*
Electrical appliance shop	Loja de electrodomésticos *<u>lo</u>-zhuh duh eh-lek-tro-doh-<u>mesh</u>-tee-koosh*
Photographer	Loja de fotografia *<u>lo</u>-zhuh duh fo-toh-gruh-<u>fee</u>-yuh*
Fashion shop	Loja de moda/boutique *<u>lo</u>-zhuh duh <u>mo</u>-duh/boo-<u>teek</u>*
Shops	Lojas *<u>loh</u>-zhuhsh*
Market	Mercado *mer-<u>ka</u>-doo*
Grocer	Mercearia *mer-see-a-<u>ree</u>-yuh*

| Mini-mart | Minimercado
mi-ni-mer-<u>ka</u>-doo |
| Jeweller | Ouriversaria/joalharia
oo-ree-ver-suh-<u>ree</u>-yuh/zhoh-al-yer-<u>ree</u>-yuh |
| Baker | Padaria
pa-duh-<u>ree</u>-yuh |
| Stationer | Papelaria
pa-pel-uh-<u>ree</u>-yuh |
| Cake shop | Pastelaria
pash-tel-a-<u>ree</u>-yuh |
| Fishmonger | Peixaria
pay-sha-<u>ree</u>-yuh |
| Perfume shop | Perfumaria
per-foo-muh-<u>ree</u>-yuh |
| Ready-to-wear | Pronto-a-vestir
<u>pron</u>-too-uh-vesh-<u>teer</u> |
| Kiosk | Quiosque
kee-<u>oshk</u> |
| Clockmaker | Relojaria
reh-lozh-uh-<u>ree</u>-yuh |
| Shoe shop | Sapataria
sa-pa-tuh-<u>ree</u>-yuh |
| Supermarket | Supermercado
soo-per-mer-<u>ka</u>-doo |
| Tobacconist | Tabacaria
ta-bah-kuh-<u>ree</u>-yuh |
| Butcher | Talho
<u>tal</u>-yoo |

GENERAL SHOPPING

| I'm just looking, thanks | Estou só a ver, obrigado/a
shtoh soh uh vair, oh-bree-<u>gah</u>-doo/uh |

I'm next	Sou eu a seguir *soh <u>ay</u>-oo uh se-<u>gheer</u>*
I'd like this	Queria isto *<u>kree</u>-uh <u>eesh</u>-too*
Can I have a look at…?	Posso ver…? *<u>poh</u>-ssoo vair…?*
Do you have…?	Tem…? *taymη…?*
…more	…mais *…mysh*
…less	…menos *…<u>may</u>-noosh*
It's rather/very expensive	É um pouco/muito caro *eh oomη <u>poh</u>-koo/<u>mweeη</u>-too <u>kah</u>-roo*
I'd like something…	Queria alguma coisa… *<u>kree</u>-uh al-<u>goo</u>-muh <u>coy</u>-suh…*
…bigger	…maior *…my-<u>or</u>*
…smaller	…mais pequena *…mysh puh-<u>kay</u>-nuh*
…cheaper	…mais barata *…mysh ba-<u>ra</u>-tuh*
Nothing else	Mais nada *mysh <u>na</u>-duh*
How much is it?	Quanto é? *<u>kwan</u>-too eh?*
Could you write it down?	Podia escrevê-lo? *po-<u>dee</u>-yuh shcre-<u>vay</u>-loo?*
Do you accept credit cards?	Aceitam cartões de crédito? *a-<u>say</u>-tamη kar-<u>toyη</u>sh duh <u>cre</u>-dee-too?*
Do you do discounts?	Fazem desconto? *<u>fa</u>-zaymη desh-<u>con</u>-too?*

Could you wrap it?	Podia embrulhá-lo?
	po-dee-yuh em-brul-ya-loo?
Do you have a bag?	Tem saco?
	taymη sa-koo?
Could you send it to...?	Podia enviá-lo para...?
	po-dee-yuh en-vee-yah-loo puh-ruh...?
One of these	Um destes
	oomη desh-tush
One of those	Um daqueles
	oomη duh-kel-ush

You may hear:

Quem é o próximo/a seguir?	Who's next?
kaymη eh oo pro-see-moo/uh se-gheer?	
Pois não?	Can I help you?
poysh nowη?	
Em que posso servi-lo?	How can I help you?
aymη kuh poh-ssoo sair-vee-loo?	
Está a ser atendido?	Are you being attended to?
shta uh sair a-ten-dee-doo?	
Não temos/não há	We don't have any/there aren't any
nowη tay-moosh/nowη ah	
Já não há	There is/are none left
zha nowη ah	
Já acabou	It has already run out
zha a-ka-boh	
Quanto quer?	How much would you like?
kwan-too kair?	
Quantos quer?	How many would you like?
kwan-toosh kair?	
Mais alguma coisa?	Anything else?
mysh al-goo-muh coy-suh?	

Que mais? *kuh mysh?*	What else?
Mais? *mysh?*	Anything more/what else?
Quer que embrulhe? *kair kuh em-<u>brul</u>-yuh?*	Do you want me to wrap it?
Quer um saco? *kair oomη <u>sa</u>-koo?*	Do you want a bag?
São (10) euros *sowη (desh) <u>air</u>-roosh*	That's (10) euros
Paga em dinheiro ou com cartão? *<u>pa</u>-guh aymη deen-<u>yay</u>-roo oh comη kar-<u>town</u>?*	Are you paying by cash or card?
Pague na caixa *pag nuh <u>kye</u>-shuh*	Pay at the till

SHOPPING FOR FOOD

Markets are an excellent place to buy cheap, fresh produce, and a great place to practise the language with the locals.

Can I have...	Dê-me... *<u>day</u>-muh...*
I'd like...	Queria... *<u>kree</u>-uh...*
...a kilo of	...um quilo de *...oomη <u>kee</u>-loo duh*
...half a kilo of	...meio quilo de *...<u>may</u>-oo <u>kee</u>-loo duh*
...(250) grams of	...(250) gramas de *...(doo-<u>zen</u>-toosh sin-<u>kwen</u>-tuh) <u>gra</u>-muhsh duh*
...a litre of	...um litro de *...oomη <u>lee</u>-troo duh*

...half a litre of	...meio litro de ..._may_-oo _lee_-troo duh
...a packet of	...um pacote de ..._oomη_ pa-_kot_ duh
...a jar of	...um pote/um frasco de ..._oomη_ pot/oomη _frash_-koo duh
...a bottle of	...uma garrafa de ..._oo_-muh guh-_ra_-fuh duh
...a box of	...uma caixa de ..._oo_-muh _kye_-shuh duh
...a tin/can of	...uma lata de ..._oo_-muh _lah_-tuh duh
...a tube of	...um tubo de ..._oomη_ _too_-boo duh
...a roll of	...um rolo de ..._oomη_ _roh_-loo duh
...a bag of	...um saco de ..._oomη_ _sa_-koo duh
...a bar of	...uma barra de ..._oo_-muh _ba_-ruh duh
...a dozen	...uma dúzia de ..._oo_-muh _doo_-zee-yuh duh
...half a dozen	...meia dúzia de ..._may_-uh _doo_-zee-yuh duh
...a slice of	...uma fatia de ..._oo_-muh fah-_tee_-yuh duh
...a bunch of (fruit)	...um cacho de ..._oomη_ _ca_-shoo duh

FRUIT AND VEGETABLES

Apple	Uma maçã _oo_-muh mah-_ssaη_

Asparagus	Espargo *shpar-goo*
Banana	Uma banana *oo-muh ba-na-nuh*
Black grapes	Uvas pretas *oo-vuhsh pre-tuhsh*
Beetroot	Beterraba *beh-teh-rah-buh*
Broccoli	Brócolos *bro-koo-loosh*
Cabbage	Uma couve *oo-muh cov*
Carrot	Uma cenoura *oo-muh se-nor-ruh*
Cauliflower	Uma couve-flor *oo-muh cov-flor*
Celery	Aipo *eye-poo*
Cucumber	Um pepino *oomη puh-pee-noo*
Fruit and vegetables	Frutas e legumes *fru-tuhsh ee leh-goomsh*
Garlic	Alho *al-yoo*
Grapefruit	Uma toranja *oo-muh toh-ran-zhuh*
Green grapes	Uvas brancas *oo-vuhsh bran-kuhsh*
Green/red pepper	Um pimento verde/vermelho *oomη pee-men-too verd/ver-mel-yoo*
Leek	Um alho-porro *oomη al-yoo-poh-roo*

Lemon	Um limão *oomη li-mown*
Lettuce	Uma alface *oo-muh al-fass*
Lime	Uma lima *oo-muh lee-muh*
Mango	Uma manga *oo-muh man-guh*
Melon	Um melão *oomη meh-lown*
Onion	Uma cebola *oo-muh se-boh-luh*
Orange	Uma laranja *oo-muh la-ran-zhuh*
Pawpaw	Uma papaia *oo-muh pa-pye-uh*
Pineapple	Um ananás *oomη a-na-nash*
Peach	Um pêssego *oomη peh-ssuh-goo*
Pear	Uma pêra *oo-muh pair-ruh*
Peas	Ervilhas *er-vil-yuhsh*
Plum	Uma ameixa *oo-muh a-may-shuh*
Potato	Uma batata *oo-muh ba-ta-tuh*
Strawberry	Um morango *oomη moh-ran-goo*
Tomato	Um tomate *oomη toh-mat*

Turnip	Um nabo *oomη na-boo*
Watercress	Agrião *a-gree-own*
Watermelon	Uma melancia *oo-muh meh-lan-see-yuh*

AT THE GROCER'S

Baby food	Alimentação para bebés *a-lee-men-ta-ssown puh-ruh beb-aysh*
Biscuits	Bolachas *bo-la-shuhsh*
Cereals	Cereais *suh-ree-aysh*
Coffee (decaffeinated)	Café (descafeinado) *kah-fay (desh-ka-fay-na-doo)*
Dog food	Comida para cães *co-mee-duh puh-ruh kyeηsh*
Eggs	Ovos *o-voosh*
Flour	Farinha *fuh-rin-yuh*
Honey	Mel *mel*
Jam	Doce *doss*
Lard	Banha *ban-yuh*
Margarine	Margarina *mar-gha-ree-nuh*
Milk...	Leite... *layt...*

...full fat	...gordo ...*gor-doo*
...semi-skimmed	...meio gordo ...*may-oo gor-doo*
...skimmed	...magro ...*ma-groo*
powdered	em pó *aymη poh*
Olive oil	Azeite (de oliva) *a-zayt (duh o-lee-vuh)*
Pasta	Massa *ma-ssuh*
Rice	Arroz *a-rozh*
Stock cubes	Cubos de caldo *koo-boosh duh cal-doo*
Sugar	Açúcar *a-ssoo-kar*
Sunflower oil	Óleo girassol *oh-lee-yoo zhee-ra-ssol*
Yoghurt	Iogurte *yo-gurt*

CHEESE

Cheese...	Queijo... ...*kay-zhoo...*
...cottage cheese	...requeijão ...*reh-kay-zhowη*
...goat's	...de cabra ...*duh ca-bruh*
...hard	...duro ...*doo-roo*

...mild	...suave ...*swav*
...sheep's	...de ovelha ...*duh o-vel-yuh*
...soft cheese like ricotta	...queijo fresco ...*kay-zhoo fresh-koo*
...strong	...forte ...*fort*

SOME REGIONAL CHEESES

Azorean cheese like Gouda	Queijo da Ilha *kay-zhoo duh il-yuh*
Cow's/ewe's milk cheese from the north	Monte *mont*
Mild cheese from Coimbra	Rabaçal *ra-ba-ssal*
Serra mountain cheese	Queijo da Serra *kay-zhoo duh sair-rah*
Strong cheese from Alentejo	Azeitão *a-zay-town*

MEAT

Bacon	Toucinho/bacon *toh-sin-yoo/bay-con*
Boiled ham	Fiambre *fee-am-bray*
Smoked ham	Presunto *pre-sun-too*
Spicy sausage	Chouriço *shoo-ree-ssoo*
Thick smoked sausage	Paio *pye-oo*

SOME SPECIALITY HAMS AND SAUSAGE MEATS

Chicken/rabbit/pork/garlic sausage	Alheiras *al-yair-uhsh*
Blood sausage made from the bladder	Bexiga *buh-shee-guh*
Pork haggis	Bucho *boo-shoo*
Liver/garlic sausage wrapped in tripe	Cacholeira *ca-shoh-lay-ruh*
Sausage from pig's belly/ breast – fried	Farinheiras *fa-rin-yair-uhsh*
Small sausages	Linguiça *lin-gwee-ssuh*
Blood sausage	Morcela *mor-seh-luh*
Large spicy sausage	Salpicão *sal-pee-kown*

AT THE BUTCHER'S

Goat	Cabrito *ka-bree-too*
Hare	Lebre *le-bruh*
Lamb	Borrego *boh-ray-goo*
Mutton	Carneiro *car-nay-roo*
Ox brain	Miolos *mee-oh-loosh*
Pig's trotters	Pezinhos de porco *pay-zeen-yoosh duh por-koo*
Pork	Carne de porco *karn duh por-koo*

Rabbit	Coelho *koh-el-yoo*
Steak	Carne de vaca *karn duh va-kuh*
Veal	Vitela *vee-teh-luh*
Wild boar	Javali *zha-vuh-lee*

CUTS

Chop	Uma costeleta *oo-muh cosh-tuh-leh-tuh*
Joint	Um quarto *oomη kwar-too*
Loin	Um lombo *oomη lom-boo*
Minced meat	Carne moída *karn moh-ee-duh*
(thin) Slice	Uma fatia *oo-muh fah-tee-yuh*
Steak	Um filete *oomη fee-let*
Without bone/fat	Sem osso/gordura *saymη o-ssoo/gor-doo-ruh*

POULTRY

Duck	Um pato *oomη pa-too*
Goose	Um ganso *oomη gan-soo*
Hen/chicken...	Uma galinha... *oo-muh ga-lin-yuh...*

...breast	...peito de galinha ..._pay_-too duh ga-_lin_-yuh
...drumsticks	...coxas ..._coh_-shuhsh
...wings	...asas ..._ah_-suhsh
...whole	...inteiro ...in-_tay_-roo
...in pieces	...em pedaços ...aymη pe-_da_-ssoosh
...large	...grande ..._grand_
...medium	...médio ..._meh_-dee-yoo
...small	...pequeno ...pe-_kay_-noo
Partridge	Um perdiz oomη per-_deezh_
Quail	Um cordoniz oomη cor-doh-_neezh_
Turkey	Um peru oomη peh-_roo_

FISH AND SEAFOOD

There is much fish and seafood to choose from in Portugal, not all of which may be familiar. It is often easier to point and ask for 'some of this or that', and ask the name of it for future reference, in case you wish to buy it again (or avoid it!).

Anchovies	Anchovas an-_shoh_-vuhsh
Clams	Ameijoas a-_may_-zho-uhsh

Crab	Caranguejo *ka-ran-gay-zhoo*
Eels	Enguias *en-ghee-uhsh*
Fish	Peixe *paysh*
Grouper	Garoupa *ga-roh-puh*
Hake	Pescada *pesh-ka-duh*
Horse mackerel	Carapau *ka-ra-powu*
Lamprey	Lampreia *lam-pray-uh*
Lobster	Lagosta *la-gosh-tuh*
Mackerel	Cavala *ka-va-luh*
Mussels	Mexilhões *meh-shil-yoynsh*
Octopus	Polvo *pol-voo*
Prawns	Gambas *gam-buhsh*
Red mullet	Salmonete *sal-moh-net*
Salmon	Salmão *sal-mown*
Salted cod	Bacalhau *ba-kal-yowu*
Sardines	Sardinhas *sar-din-yuhsh*
Scabbard fish	Peixe espada *paysh shpa-duh*

Sea bream	Dourada
	duh-ra-duh
Shrimp	Camarão
	ka-ma-rown
Sole	Linguado
	lin-gwa-doo
Squid/cuttlefish	Choquinhos/lulas
	shoh-keen-yoosh/loo-luhsh
Swordfish	Espadarte
	shpa-dart
Trout	Truta
	tru-tuh
Tuna	Atum
	a-toomη
Please could you...?	Podia..., por favor?
	po-dee-yuh..., por fa-vor?
...clean it	...limpá-lo
	...lim-pa-loo
...fillet it	...preparar em filetes
	...pre-puh-rar aymη fee-let-esh
...take the bones out	...tirar as espinhas
	...ti-rar uhsh shpin-yuhsh
...remove the head	...tirar a cabeça
	...ti-rar uh ka-bay-suh

AT THE BAKER'S

It is not always entirely clear where a baker's may be located, as many do not have proper shop fronts. However, the smell of fresh bread wafting from an open doorway may give you a clue; often the baker's is simply a single, dark room, with a small counter and a few shelves of items. If you are not there early, you will miss the delight of warm, fresh bread.

Bread	Pão *powη*
Bread roll	Um pãozinho/um papo-seco *oomη powη-<u>zeen</u>-yoo/oomη <u>pa</u>-poo-<u>se</u>-koo*
(6) Bread rolls	(6) Pãezinhos *(saysh) pyeη-<u>zeen</u>-yoosh*
Loaf	Uma carcaça/um pão *<u>oo</u>-muh kar-<u>ka</u>-suh/oomη powη*
...large	...grande *...grand*
...medium	...média *...<u>meh</u>-dee-yuh*
...small	...pequena *...puh-<u>kay</u>-nuh*
Long loaf/baguette	Um cacete *oomη ka-<u>sset</u>*
Sliced bread	Pão de forma *powη duh <u>for</u>-muh*

TYPICAL PORTUGUESE BREAD

Broa *<u>broh</u>-uh*	Maize bread
Folhada *fol-<u>ya</u>-duh*	Bread with meats cooked in it
Pão de chouriço *powη duh shoo-<u>ree</u>-ssoo*	Bread with spicy sausage baked in it
Pão de milho *powη duh <u>mil</u>-yoo*	Corn bread

CAKES AND SWEETS

Cake...	Um bolo de... *oomη boh-loo duh...*
...chocolate	...chocolate *...sho-ko-lat*
...almond	...amêndoa *...a-men-doh-uh*
Chewy sweets	Caramelos *ka-ra-meh-loosh*
Chocolates	Chocolates *sho-ko-la-tesh*
Lollipop	Uma chupa-chupa *oo-muh shoo-puh-shoo-puh*
Mints	Balas de hortelã *ba-luhsh duh or-tuh-laη*
Pastry	Um pastel *oomη pash-tel*
Sweets	Rebuçados/balas *re-boo-ssah-doosh/ba-luhsh*
Tart	Uma tarte *oo-muh tart*

SOME TYPICAL PORTUGUESE CAKES

Bola de Berlim *boh-luh duh ber-limη*	Cream-filled doughnut/bun
Bolo de creme *boh-loo duh crem*	Custard-cream filled cake
Bolo Rei *boh-loo ray*	Sponge with dried fruits, to be eaten at Christmas
Mil folhas *mil fol-yuhsh*	Mille feuille
Pastel de nata/de Belém *pash-tel duh na-tuh/duh beh-laymη*	Small custard-cream cake

Suspiros *suss-pee-roosh*	Small meringues

ICE CREAM

Ice cream...	Um gelado de... *oomη zhuh-lah-doo duh...*
...vanilla	...baunilha *...bowu-nil-yuh*
...strawberry	...morango *...moh-ran-goo*
...orange	...laranja *...la-ran-zhuh*
Ice lolly	Um picolé *oomη pi-ko-lay*
What flavours do you have?	Quais sabores tem? *kwysh sa-bor-esh taymη?*
Do you have this one?	Tem este? *taymη esht?*
2 of those, please	2 daqueles, por favor *doysh duh-kel-uhsh, por fa-vor*

AT THE TOBACCONIST'S, NEWSAGENT'S, BOOKSHOP

On-street kiosks sell newspapers, cigarettes, stamps and postcards, as do tobacconists' shops and small newsagents.

Tourist areas sell the main newspapers from Britain, Germany, the Netherlands and Spain.

Books can be quite expensive, especially those translated or imported from abroad. However, there are also many bargains to be found in smaller shops, should you wish to try reading some Portuguese. There is a good range of magazines, comics, puzzle books and school textbooks, all of which would make an ideal starting point.

Box of matches	Uma caixa de fósforos *oo-muh <u>kye</u>-shuh duh <u>foss</u>-foh-roosh*
Cigars	Charutos *sha-<u>roo</u>-toosh*
Lighter	Um isqueiro *oomη ish-<u>kay</u>-roo*
Packet of cigarettes	Um maço de cigarros *oomη <u>ma</u>-ssoo duh see-<u>gah</u>-roosh*
Pipe	Um cachimbo *oomη ka-<u>shim</u>-boo*
Tobacco	Tabaco *ta-<u>ba</u>-koo*
Do you have any postcards?	Tem postais? *taymη posh-<u>tysh</u>?*
Do you sell stamps?	Vende selos? *vend <u>se</u>-loosh?*
I'd like...	Queria... *<u>kree</u>-uh...*
...a daily paper	...um (jornal) diário *...oomη (zhor-<u>nal</u>) dee-<u>ah</u>-ree-yoo*
...an English paper	...um jornal inglês *...oomη zhor-<u>nal</u> in-<u>glaysh</u>*
...a magazine in Portuguese	...uma revista em português *...<u>oo</u>-muh reh-<u>vish</u>-tuh aymη por-too-<u>gaysh</u>*
...a town plan	...um plano da cidade *...oomη <u>pla</u>-noo duh see-<u>da</u>-duh*
...a map of the region	...um mapa da região *...oomη <u>ma</u>-puh duh re-zhee-<u>own</u>*
...a book about	...um livro sobre *...oomη <u>lee</u>-vroo <u>so</u>-bray*

AT THE CHEMIST'S

The International Green Cross symbol is used to denote a
pharmacy (*Farmácia*).

Chemists on duty out of hours are listed in shop windows and
in the local paper.

The pharmacy is the first point of call for people with minor
ailments. See also page 123.

I'd like something for...	Queria alguma coisa para... *kree-uh al-goo-muh coy-suh puh-ruh...*
Do you have something for...?	Tem alguma coisa para...? *taymη al-goo-muh coy-suh puh-ruh...?*
...a sore throat	...dor de garganta *...dor duh gar-gan-tuh*
...headache	...dor de cabeça *...dor duh ka-bay-suh*
...tummy ache	...dor de estômago *...dor duh shtoh-muh-goo*
...nausea	...o enjoo *...oo en-zhoh*
...a hangover	...uma ressaca *...oo-muh re-ssa-kuh*

See also page 110 on health.

I have this prescription	Tenho esta receita *tayn-yoo eh-shtuh re-say-tuh*
Do you have the same brand?	Tem a mesma marca? *taymη uh mezh-muh mar-kuh?*
I usually take...	Normalmente tomo... *nor-mal-ment toh-moo...*

How often should I take it?	Quantas vezes devo tomá-lo? _kwan_-tuhsh _vay_-zesh _day_-voo toh-_ma_-loo?
Is it safe for me to drive?	Posso conduzir? _poh_-ssoo con-doo-_zeer_?
I'm allergic to...	Sou alérgico/a a... soh a-_ler_-zhee-koo/uh uh...
I need...	Preciso de... pruh-_see_-soo duh...
...insect repellent	...repelente contra insectos ...re-puh-_lent_ _con_-truh in-_sek_-toosh
...plasters	...adesivos/pensos ...a-duh-_see_-voosh/_pen_-soosh
...throat pastilles/syrup	...pastilhas/xarope ...pash-_til_-yuhsh/sha-_rop_
...sun cream	...creme solar ...crem soh-_lar_
...aspirin/parecetamol	...aspirina/parecetemol ...ash-puh-_ree_-nuh/pa-re-_se_-te-mol
...eye drops	...colírio ...co-_lee_-ree-yoo
...sanitary towels	...pensos higiénicos ..._pen_-soosh ee-zhee-_en_-ee-koosh
...a bandage	...uma ligadura ..._oo_-muh li-ga-_du_-ruh
...cotton wool	...algodão ...al-go-_down_
...ointment	...pomada ...po-_ma_-duh
...tablets for	...comprimidos para ...com-pree-_mee_-doosh _puh_-ruh
...the pill	...a pílula ...uh _pi_-loo-luh

GENERAL TOILETRIES

Aftershave	Loção para depois da barba *lo-<u>sow</u>ŋ <u>puh</u>-ruh de-<u>poysh</u> duh <u>bar</u>-buh*
Deodorant	Desodorizante *des-oh-doh-ree-<u>zant</u>*
Lipsalve	Pomada para os lábios *po-<u>ma</u>-duh <u>puh</u>-ruh oosh <u>la</u>-bee-yoosh*
Lipstick	Batom *ba-<u>tom</u>ŋ*
Make-up	Maquilhagem *ma-kil-<u>ya</u>-zhemŋ*
Make-up remover	Desmaquilhante *desh-mak-il-<u>yant</u>*
Moisturiser cream	Creme hidrante *crem ee-<u>drant</u>*
Paper tissues	Lenços de papel *<u>len</u>-ssoosh duh puh-<u>pel</u>*
Perfume	Perfume *per-<u>foom</u>*
Razor blades	Lâminas de barba *<u>la</u>-mee-nuhsh duh <u>bar</u>-buh*
Shampoo	Champó *sham-<u>poh</u>*
Shaving cream	Creme para barbear *crem <u>puh</u>-ruh bar-bee-<u>yar</u>*
Shower gel/bubble bath	Gel duche/banho de espuma *zhel doosh/<u>ban</u>-yoo duh <u>shpoo</u>-muh*
Soap	Sabão *sa-<u>bow</u>ŋ*
Talcum powder	Pó de talco *poh duh <u>tal</u>-koo*

Toothbrush	Escova de dentes
	shco-vuh duh den-tesh
Toothpaste	Pasta dentífrica
	pash-tuh den-ti-fri-kuh

HOUSEHOLD ITEMS

Conditioner	Amaciador de roupa
	a-ma-see-a-dor duh roh-puh
Disinfectant	Disinfectante
	dis-in-fek-tant
Duster	Um pano do pó
	oomŋ pa-noo doo poh
Rubbish bags	Sacos para o lixo
	sa-koosh puh-ruh oo lee-shoo
Scouring pad	Um esfregão
	oomŋ shfre-gowŋ
Tea towel	Um pano da loiça
	oomŋ pa-noo duh loy-ssuh
Toilet paper	Papel higiénico
	puh-pel ee-zhee-yen-ee-koo
Washing powder	Detergente máquina roupa
	de-ter-zhent ma-kee-nuh roh-puh
Washing-up cloth	Um pano para lavar loiça
	oomŋ pa-noo puh-ruh luh-var loy-ssuh
Washing-up liquid	Detergente líquido para loiça
	de-ter-zhent li-kee-doo puh-ruh loy-ssuh

CAMPING, AT THE BEACH

Do you sell...?	Vende...?
	vend...?
...tent pegs	...estacas de tenda
	...shta-kuhsh duh ten-duh

...ground sheets	...oleados *...oh-lee-ya-doosh*
...repair kits	...caixas de remendos *...kye-shuhsh duh re-men-doosh*
...sleeping bags	...sacos de dormir *...sa-koosh duh dor-meer*
...insecticide	...repelente *...re-puh-lent*
What equipment do you have?	Que equipamento tem? *Kay eh-kee-pa-men-too taymη?*
Do you hire out...?	Aluga...? *A-loo-guh...?*
...tents	...tendas *...ten-duhsh*
...cooking equipment	...utensílios para cozinhar *...u-ten-sil-ee-yoosh puh-ruh koh-zin-yar*
...sunshades	...toldos/chapéus de sol *...tol-doosh/sha-pay-oosh duh sol*
How much is it to hire a beach tent?	Quanto é para alugar uma barraca? *kwan-too eh puh-ruh a-loo-gar oo-muh ba-ra-kuh?*
Where do we hire...?	Onde alugamos...? *ond a-loo-ga-moosh...?*
...a sun bed?	...uma espreguiçadeira? *...oo-muh shpre-ghee-ssa-day-ruh?*
...a beach towel	...uma toalha de praia *...oo-muh toh-al-yuh duh pra-yuh*
...a beach ball	...uma bola de praia *...oo-muh boh-luh duh pra-yuh*
...a freezer bag	...uma geladeira *...oo-muh zheh-la-day-ruh*

PHOTOGRAPHIC

Films are readily available in the Algarve, in all the shops selling general tourist products, and in stationery shops and photographers' elsewhere in Portugal. There are some specialist photography shops, which also offer quick developing.

Photographic materials are generally more expensive in Portugal than in the UK.

Film...	Um...rolo/filme
	oomη..._roh_-loo/film
...black and white	...a preto e branco
	...uh _pray_-too ee _bran_-koo
...colour	...a cores
	...uh _cor_-esh
...for slides	para diapositivas
	puh-ruh dee-uh-po-see-_tee_-vuhsh
...for a video camera	para filmar
	*_puh_-ruh fil-_mar_*
Please could you...?	Por favor, podia...?
	Por fa-_vor_, po-_dee_-yuh...?
...develop the film	...revelar o rolo
	...re-veh-_lar_ oo _roh_-loo
...load the camera	...colocar o rolo na máquina
	...coh-lo-_kar_ oo _roh_-loo nuh _ma_-kee-nuh
...take the film out	...tirar o rolo
	...ti-_rar_ oo _roh_-loo
...repair the camera	...consertar a máquina
	...con-ser-_tar_ uh _ma_-kee-nuh
The film is stuck	O rolo está preso
	Oo _roh_-loo shta _preh_-soo
It's not working	Não funciona
	nowη fun-ssee-_oh_-nuh

I need new batteries	Preciso de pilhas novas *pruh-<u>see</u>-soo duh <u>pil</u>-yuhsh <u>noh</u>-vuhsh*
When will they be ready?	Quando estarão prontas? *<u>kwan</u>-doo shta-<u>rown</u> <u>pron</u>-tuhsh?*

CLOTHES

Clothing can range from the very cheap, at the *feira* markets, to the ludicrously expensive in the new ultra-chic boutiques of Lisbon and Porto.

Northern Portugal has long been a hive of the textile industry, and it now accommodates a number of factory outlets.

Blouse	A blusa *uh <u>blu</u>-suh*
Bra	O soutien *oo su-tee-<u>ann</u>*
Clothes	Roupa *<u>roh</u>-puh*
Coat	O casaco *oo ka-<u>sa</u>-koo*
Dress	O vestido *oo vesh-<u>tee</u>-doo*
Jeans	Os jeans/as calças de ganga *oosh jeans/uhsh <u>kal</u>-ssuhsh duh <u>gan</u>-guh*
Jumper	O pulover *oo pul-<u>o</u>-ver*
Knickers/pants	As cuecas *uhsh <u>kweh</u>-kuhsh*
Overcoat	O sobretudo *oo soh-bray-<u>too</u>-doo*

Pyjamas	O pijama *oo pi-zha-muh*
Shirt	A camisa *uh ca-mee-suh*
Shorts	Os calções *oosh kal-ssoynsh*
Skirt	A saia *uh sy-uh*
Socks	As meias/as peúgas *uhsh may-uhsh/uhsh pay-oo-guhsh*
Suit	O fato *oo fa-too*
Sweater	A camisola *uh ka-mee-soh-luh*
Swimsuit	O fato de banho *oo fa-too duh ban-yoo*
Tie	A gravata *uh gra-va-tuh*
Tights	Os collants *oosh co-lann*
Tracksuit	O fato de treino *oo fa-too duh tray-noo*
Trousers	As calças *uhsh kal-ssuhsh*
T-shirt	A T-shirt *uh T-shirt*
Underwear	A roupa interior *uh roh-puh in-teh-ree-yor*
I'd like size 38	Queria tamanho 38 *kree-uh ta-man-yoo 38*
Can I try it/them on?	Posso provar/experimentar? *poh-ssoo pro-var/shpe-ree-men-tar?*

Where is the fitting room?	Onde é o gabinete de provas? *ond eh oo ga-bee-<u>net</u> duh <u>pro</u>-vuhsh?*
It's too small/big/tight	É muito pequeno/grande/apertado *eh <u>mween</u>-too pe-<u>kay</u>-noo/grand/a-per-<u>ta</u>-doo*
Do you have larger/smaller?	Tem maior/mais pequeno? *taymη my-<u>or</u>/mysh pe-<u>kay</u>-noo?*
Do you have in...?	Tem em...? *taymη aymη...?*
...blue	...azul *...a-<u>zool</u>*
...green	...verde *...verd*
...brown	...castanho *...cash-<u>tan</u>-yoo*
...red	...encarnado/vermelho *...en-kar-<u>nah</u>-doo/ver-<u>mel</u>-yoo*
...white	...branco *...<u>bran</u>-koo*
...black	...preto *...<u>pray</u>-too*
...pink	...rosa *...<u>ro</u>-suh*
...yellow	...amarelo *...a-ma-<u>reh</u>-loo*
...purple	...roxo *...<u>ro</u>-shoo*
...orange	...laranja *...la-<u>ran</u>-zhuh*
light/dark...	...claro/escuro *...<u>cla</u>-roo/<u>shcoo</u>-roo*
Do you have in other colours?	Tem noutras cores? *taymη <u>noh</u>-truhsh <u>cor</u>-esh?*

with/without...	com/sem... _com_η/sайm_η...
...stripes	...riscas ..._rish_-kuhsh
...a pattern	...estampado ...shtam-_pa_-doo
...dots	...bolinhas ...bo-_lin_-yuhsh
...check	...quadrados/xadrez ...kwa-_dra_-doosh/sha-_drezh_
...pockets	...bolsos ..._bol_-soosh
in...	em... _aym_η...
...cotton	...algodão ...al-go-_down_
...silk	...seda ..._say_-duh
...wool	...lã ..._la_η
...linen	...linho ..._lin_-yoo
...leather	...cabedal/pele ...ka-beh-_dal_/pel
...velvet	...veludo ...ve-_lu_-doo
...satin	...cetim ...se-_tim_η
Does it/they suit me?	Fica/Ficam-me bem? _fee_-kuh/_fee_-kamη-muh baymη?
I'll take this	Levo isto _lay_-voo _eesh_-too

There's one in the window
Há um/uma na montra
ah oomη/<u>oo</u>-muh nuh <u>mon</u>-truh

I don't like this one
Não gosto deste
nowη <u>gosh</u>-too desht

I prefer that one
Prefiro aquele
pruh-<u>fee</u>-roo a-<u>kel</u>

Can I change it if it doesn't fit?
Posso trocar se não servir?
<u>poh</u>-ssoo tro-<u>kar</u> suh nowη ser-<u>veer</u>?

SHOES AND SHOE REPAIRS

Shoes made in Portugal are of good quality and reasonably priced.
Shoes shops are aplenty, and you can also find bargains at the
feira markets.
Shoe repair shops are called *sapateiros*.
In Lisbon, in particular, you can still have your shoes polished in
the street.

Have you got these in blue?
Tem estes em azul?
taymη <u>esh</u>-tesh aymη a-<u>zool</u>?

Are they leather?
São de couro?
sowη duh <u>cor</u>-oo?

These are too tight
Estes apertam muito
<u>esh</u>-tesh a-<u>per</u>-tamη <u>mween</u>-too

These are too big
Estes são muito grandes
<u>esh</u>-tesh sowη <u>mween</u>-too <u>gran</u>-desh

Can I see...?
Posso ver...?
<u>poh</u>-ssoo vair...?

...sandals
...sandálias
...san-<u>da</u>-lee-yuhsh

...beach shoes/flipflops
...chinelas de praia
...shee-<u>nel</u>-uhsh duh <u>pra</u>-yuh

...high-heeled/flat shoes	...sapatos de salto alto/sem salto
	...sa-__pa__-toosh duh __sal__-too __al__-too/saymη __sal__-too
...boots	...botas
	...__boh__-tuhsh
...trainers	...ténis
	...__te__-nish
Can you repair these shoes?	Pode consertar estes sapatos?
	pod con-ser-__tar__ esh-tesh sa-__pa__-toosh?
Can you put on a new sole/heel?	Pode pôr uma sola nova/um salto novo?
	pod por __oo__-muh __soh__-luh __noh__-vuh/oomη __sal__-too noh-voo?
When will they be ready?	Quando estarão prontos?
	__kwan__-doo shta-__rown__ pron-toosh?
How much will it cost?	Quanto vai custar?
	__kwan__-too vye cush-__tar__?
Do you have shoe polish?	Tem pomada?
	taymη po-__ma__-duh?
Shoelaces	Cordões
	cor-__doyη__sh

BANKS AND POST OFFICES

Most banks open from 8.30am to 3pm, except in tourist areas where they often have extended hours. Most banks have cash machine areas, where you have to swipe your card through an electronic door device. Automatic cash machines, called *multibancos*, are everywhere now, and you can carry out a range of services at them, including withdrawing cash with your own cash card. Instructions on-screen give you a choice of language, but after each step of the process, remember to press the green button (*continuar*) to move on to the next instruction.

If you need to change travellers' cheques, make sure you have your passport with you; you will also be asked where you are staying in Portugal, so have the details to hand. Some larger hotels also exchange cheques, although the rate will be less favourable than in the banks or *câmbio* shops (exchange bureaux).

When you are being served at the bank, you will probably be dealt with by one clerk, who may then send you to collect your money from the cash till (*caixa*), which is usually further down the counter. Portugal was one of the first EU states to sign up to the euro, and it has now been in circulation there since its inception. Work out your own exchange-rate table before you go, to avoid confusion.

You may see:

Caixa	Cash desk
Caixa automático	Cash machine
Câmbio	Exchange
Cheque	Cheque
Compra	Buy
Cotação/câmbio	Exchange rate
Nota	Note
Moeda	Cash
Multibanco	Cash machine
Venda	Sell

BANK

I'd like to change…	Queria trocar… *kree-uh tro-kar…*
…these pounds (sterling)	…estas libras (esterlinas) *…esh-tuhsh lee-bruhsh (shter-lee-nuhsh)*
…these dollars	…estes dólares *…esh-tesh doh-la-resh*

...this into euros	...isto em euros ..._eesh_-too aym_η_ _air_-roosh
...this into pounds	...isto em libras ..._eesh_-too aym_η_ _lee_-bruhsh
...this into dollars	...isto em dólares ..._eesh_-too aym_η_ _doh_-la-resh
I have (100) pounds	Tenho (100) libras _tayn_-yoo (saym_η_) _lee_-bruhsh
There are (200) dollars	Há (200) dólares ah (doo-_zen_-toosh) _doh_-la-resh

For numbers, see page 183.

I'd like to cash...	Queria trocar... _kree_-uh tro-_kar_...
...these traveller's cheques	...estes cheques de viagem ..._esh_-tesh _sheh_-kush duh vee-_a_-zhem_η_
...these eurocheques	...estes eurocheques ..._esh_-tesh air-roo-_shek_-esh
...this cheque	...este cheque ..._esht shek_
What is the current exchange rate?	A como é o câmbio actual? uh _com_-oo eh oo _cam_-bee-yoo ac-too-_al_?
How much commission do you charge?	Cobra quanta comissão? _coh_-bruh _kwan_-tuh coh-mee-_sown_?
Do you want...?	Quer...? _Kair_...?
...my passport	...o meu passaporte ...oo _may_-oo pass-uh-_port_
...my Eurocheque card	...o meu cartão Eurocheque ...oo _may_-oo kar-_town_ air-roo-_shek_

Where do I sign?	Onde é que assino? *ond eh kuh a-<u>see</u>-noo?*
Could you give me...	Podia dar-me... *po-<u>dee</u>-yuh <u>dar</u>-muh...*
...small notes	...notas pequenas *...<u>noh</u>-tuhsh peh-<u>kay</u>-nuhsh*
...coins	...moedas *...moh-<u>ay</u>-duhsh*
...small change	...dinheiro trocado *...deen-<u>yay</u>-roo tro-<u>ka</u>-doo*
...(5) euro coins	...moedas de (5) euros *...moh-<u>ay</u>-duhsh duh (<u>sin</u>-koo) <u>air</u>-roosh*
Can I use this card?	Posso usar este cartão? *<u>poh</u>-ssoo oo-<u>sar</u> esht kar-<u>town</u>?*
Could you call my bank?	Podia telefonar ao meu banco? *po-<u>dee</u>-yuh te-le-fo-<u>nar</u> ow <u>may</u>-oo <u>ban</u>-koo?*
Has some money arrived for me?	Chegou uma transferência para mim? *shay-<u>goh</u> <u>oo</u>-muh trans-feh-<u>ren</u>-see-yuh <u>puh</u>-ruh meemη?*
I've lost...	Perdi... *per-<u>dee</u>...*
...some traveller's cheques	...alguns cheques de viagem *...al-<u>goonsh</u> <u>sheh</u>-kush duh vee-<u>a</u>-zhemη*
...some Eurocheques	...alguns Eurocheques *...al-<u>goonsh</u> air-roo-<u>shek</u>-esh*
...my (credit) card	...o meu cartão (de crédito) *...oo <u>may</u>-oo kar-<u>town</u> (duh <u>cre</u>-dee-too)*
...my cheque book	...o meu talão de cheques *...oo <u>may</u>-oo ta-<u>lown</u> duh <u>sheh</u>-kesh*

The machine has eaten my card	A máquina guardou o meu cartão *uh ma-kee-nuh gwar-doh oo may-oo kar-town*
The machine is not working	A máquina está avariada *uh ma-kee-nuh shta a-va-ree-a-duh*
Is there another cash machine near here?	Há outro multibanco perto daqui? *ah oh-troo mul-tee-ban-koo per-too duh-key?*
How does this work?	Como funciona isto? *com-oo fun-ssee-oh-nuh eesh-too?*
I'd like to...	Queria... *kree-uh...*
...open a savings account	...abrir uma conta a prazo *...a-breer oo-muh con-tuh uh pra-zoo*
...open a current account	...abrir uma conta à ordem *...a-breer oo-muh con-tuh a or-demη*
...pay this into my account	...depositar isto na minha conta *...de-po-see-tar eesh-too nuh meen-yuh con-tuh*
...withdraw (200) euros from my account	...levantar (200) euros da minha conta *...le-van-tar (doo-zen-toosh) air-roosh duh meen-yuh con-tuh*
...transfer some money	...transferir algum dinheiro *...trans-fuh-reer al-goomη deen-yay-roo*
...send a giro	...mandar um cheque de correio *...man-dar oomη shek duh koh-ray-oo*
...pay these bills	...pagar estas contas *puh-gar esh-tuhsh con-tuhsh*

...check the balance of my account
...ver o saldo da minha conta
...*vair oo sal-doo duh meen-yuh con-tuh*

...speak with the manager
...falar com o gerente
...*fa-lar comη oo zheh-rent*

Here is/are...
Aqui tem...
a-key taymη...

...the details
...os detalhes
...*oosh day-tal-yuhsh*

...my residence permit
...a minha residência
...*uh meen-yuh re-see-den-see-yuh*

...my documents
...os meus documentos
...*oosh may-oosh doh-ku-men-toosh*

...my bank card
...o meu cartão do banco
...*oo may-oo kar-town doo ban-koo*

You may hear:

Quer assinar aqui?
kair a-ssin-ar a-key?

Can you sign here?

Seu passaporte, por favor
say-yoo pass-uh-port, por fa-vor

Your passport, please

Podia passar para a caixa?
po-dee-yuh pa-ssar puh-ruh uh kye-shuh?

Could you go to the till/cash desk?

Isto é para o senhor/a senhora
eesh-too eh puh-ruh oo sehn-your/ uh sehn-your-uh

This is for you

Podia...?
po-dee-yuh...?

Could you...?

...esperar um momento
...*shpe-rar oomη mo-men-too*

...wait a moment

...preencher isto ..._pray-en-shair ish-too_	...fill this in
...sentar um bocadinho ..._sen-tar oomη boh-ka-din-yoo_	...sit down a short while
...confirmar a sua morada ..._con-feer-mar uh soo-uh mo-ra-duh_	...confirm your address
...mostrar-me ..._mosh-trar-muh_	...show me
Como se chama? _com-oo suh sha-muh?_	What is your name?
Morada aqui em Portugal? _mo-ra-duh a-key aymη por-too-gal?_	Your address here in Portugal?

POST OFFICE

Look for the sign _Correios_ and the CTT sign (_Correios, Telégrafos e Telefones_).

Post offices open usually 8.30am–6/6.30pm, Monday to Friday, and later in major cities.

There are automatic stamp machines with instructions in different languages in some town squares, airports and bus and train stations. You can also buy stamps at _quiosques_ (on-street kiosks), _tabacarias_ (newsagents/tobacconists) and in some hotels.

Inside the post office, look for the sign _Selos_ (stamps).

Some post offices also have telephoning services, although you will pay a higher rate to be connected via an operator.

A stamp for England/the United States	Um selo para a Inglaterra/os Estados Unidos _oomη seh-loo puh-ruh uh in-gla-tair-ruh/oosh shta-doosh oo-nee-doosh_

Three (2) euro stamps	Três selos de (2) euros *Traysh seh-loosh duh (doysh) air-roosh*
I'd like to send...	Queria enviar... *kree-uh en-vee-ar...*
...this letter	...esta carta *...eh-shtuh car-tuh*
...this parcel	...esta encomenda *...eh-shtuh en-ko-men-duh*
...this postcard	...este postal *...esht posh-tal*
...some money	...dinheiro *...deen-yay-roo*
By airmail	Por correio aéreo/por avião *por koh-ray-oo a-eh-ree-oo/por a-vee-yown*
By surface mail	Por correio terrestre/via superfície *por koh-ray-oo teh-resht/vee-uh soo-per-fee-see-eh*
First class (priority)	Por correio azul *por koh-ray-oo a-zool*
By registered post	Registado *re-zhees-ta-doo*
Proof of delivery	Prova de entrega *proh-vuh duh en-tray-guh*
Special delivery (insured)	Valor declarado *va-lor de-kla-ra-doo*
Postal order	Vale de correio *val duh koh-ray-oo*
Inland	Para o interior *puh-ruh oo in-teh-ree-or*
Overseas	Para o estrangeiro *puh-ruh oo shtran-zhay-roo*

Is there a parcel for me?	Há uma encomenda para mim? *ah oo-muh en-ko-men-duh puh-ruh meemη?*
I'd like a post-office box	Queria um apartado *kree-uh oomη a-par-ta-doo*
How long will it take to arrive?	Quanto tempo leva para chegar? *kwan-too tem-poo lay-vuh puh-ruh shuh-gar?*
I'd like to make a phone call	Queria fazer uma chamada *kree-uh fa-zair oo-muh sha-ma-duh*

YOU MAY SEE:

Caixa de correio	Postbox
Correio azul	Priority post
Encomendas	Parcels
Estrangeiro	Overseas
Guichet	Counter
Horas de abertura/horário	Opening hours
Horas de recolha/tiragem	Collection times
Posta Restante	Poste-restante
Selos	Stamps
Telegramas	Telegrams
Vales postais	Money orders

You may hear:

É aquele guichet *eh a-kel ghee-shay*	It's that window/counter
Preencha esta ficha/este formulário *pray-en-shuh eh-shtuh fee-shuh/esht for-moo-la-ree-yoo*	Fill in this form

Ponha a morada aqui
pon-yuh uh mo-ra-duh a-key

Put the address here

Não pode enviá-lo assim
*nown pod en-vee-yah-loo
a-sseemn*

You can't send it like that

Ponha na balança
Pon-yuh nuh bah-lan-ssuh

Put it on the weighing scales

Cabine número (5)
ka-been noo-muh-roo (sin-koo)

Booth number (5) [telephone]

Aguarde um momento
a-gward oomn mo-men-too

Wait a minute

Está impedido
shta im-peh-dee-doo

It's engaged

Ninguém atende
nin-gaymn a-tend

No one's answering

COMMUNICATIONS

TELEPHONE

Telephone kiosks and booths have clear instructions on how to use them in a range of languages, plus dialling codes for a number of countries.

Although most modern telephones are card-operated, with cards available from Telecom shops, street kiosks and tobacconists, many still use coins, especially those in small bars and cafés. You can also make calls at many post offices and Portugal Telecom shops, where you will be connected through an operator – these can work out a lot more expensive, as do calls made from hotels.

Mobile phone-ownership is massive in Portugal – check first with your own company to see if it will work overseas.

To phone the UK from Portugal, first dial 00-44-.

Is there a phone box near here?	Há uma cabine telefónica perto daqui? *ah <u>oo</u>-muh ka-<u>been</u> te-le-<u>foh</u>-nee-kuh <u>per</u>-too duh-<u>key</u>?*
Can I use the phone?	Posso usar o telefone? *<u>poh</u>-ssoo oo-<u>sar</u> oo te-le-<u>fon</u>?*
Do you have a phone?	Tem telefone? *taymη te-le-<u>fon</u>?*
Do you have a phone book?	Tem uma lista telefónica? *taymη <u>oo</u>-muh <u>lish</u>-tuh te-le-<u>foh</u>-nee-kuh?*
...yellow pages	...páginas amarelas *...<u>pa</u>-zhee-nuhsh a-ma-<u>ray</u>-luhsh*
What is the code for (Manchester)?	Qual é o indicativo para (Manchester)? *kwal eh oo in-dee-ka-<u>tee</u>-voo <u>puh</u>-ruh (Manchester)?*
Can I speak to...?	Posso falar com...? *<u>poh</u>-ssoo fa-<u>lar</u> comη...?*
Could I have extension...	Queria a extensão... *<u>kree</u>-uh uh shten-<u>sown</u>...*
I'll call back later	Telefono mais tarde *te-le-<u>foh</u>-noo mysh tard*
Hello (on getting through)	Está?/Está lá? *shta?/shta la?*
It's (Mr Brown) – formal	O meu nome é (Mr Brown) *oo <u>may</u>-oo nom eh (Mr Brown)*
It's (Jane Black) – informal	Daqui fala (Jane Black) *duh-<u>key</u> <u>fa</u>-luh (Jane Black)*
Can I leave a message?	Posso deixar um recado? *<u>poh</u>-ssoo day-<u>shar</u> oomη re-<u>ka</u>-doo?*
Can you ask him/her to call me?	Pode pedir-lhe para me chamar? *pod pe-<u>deer</u>-lyuh <u>puh</u>-ruh me sha-<u>mar</u>?*

My number is...	O meu número é... *oo may-oo noo-muh-roo eh...*
I'm sorry, I've got the wrong number	Desculpe, enganei-me no número *desh-koolp, en-gan-ay-muh noo noo-muh-roo*
Goodbye (on replacing receiver)	Com licença *comη lee-sen-suh*

TALKING TO THE OPERATOR

I'd like to make a reverse-charge call	Queria fazer uma chamada a cobrar no destino *kree-uh fa-zair oo-muh sha-ma-duh uh co-brar noo desh-tee-noo*
Could you...?	Podia...? *po-dee-yuh...*
...connect me to	...ligar-me com *...lee-gar-muh comη*
...give me the number of	...dar-me o número de *...dar-muh oo noo-muh-roo duh...*
...tell me the cost of the call	...dizer-me o custo da chamada *...dee-zair-muh oo cush-too duh sha-ma-duh*
I've been cut off	Fomos cortados *fo-moosh cor-ta-doosh*
Can I pay by card?	Posso pagar com cartão? *poh-ssoo puh-gar comη kar-towη?*

ANSWERING THE PHONE

| Hello | Estou (sim)
shtoh (seemη) |
| It's me | Sou eu,...
soh ay-oo,... |

This is…

Daqui fala…
duh-<u>key</u> <u>fa</u>-luh…

One moment, please

Um momento, por favor
oomη mo-<u>men</u>-too, por fa-<u>vor</u>

You may hear:

Há uma chamada para você
ah <u>oo</u>-muh sha-<u>ma</u>-duh <u>puh</u>-ruh voh-<u>say</u>

There is a call for you

Não está
nowη shta

He/She is not here

Está numa reunião
shta <u>noo</u>-muh ray-oo-nee-<u>own</u>

He/She is in a meeting

Quer deixar um recado?
kair day-<u>shar</u> oomη re-<u>ka</u>-doo?

Do you want to leave a message?

Enganou-se no número
en-ga-<u>noh</u>-suh noo <u>noo</u>-muh-roo

You have the wrong number

Qual é o seu número?
kwal eh oo <u>say</u>-oo <u>noo</u>-muh-roo?

What is your number?

Qual é o indicativo da cidade?
kwal eh oo in-dee-ka-<u>tee</u>-voo duh see-<u>da</u>-duh?

What is the local code?

Com quem quer falar?
comη kaymη kair fa-<u>lar</u>?

Who do you want to speak to?

Não desligue
nowη desh-<u>leeg</u>

Don't hang up

Não atende
nowη a-<u>tend</u>

There's no answer

Está impedido/Está a falar
shta im-peh-<u>dee</u>-doo/shta uh fa-<u>lar</u>

It's engaged

Pode falar
pod fa-<u>lar</u>

You can speak now

Espere um momento *shpair oom*η *mo-men-too*	Wait a moment
Volto a tentar mais tarde *vol-too uh ten-tar mysh tard*	I'll try again later

ELECTRONIC

There are a few Internet cafés now, mostly in the larger cities and in the Algarve, where you can expect a range of communication facilities. Faxes can also be sent from some commercial businesses in the Algarve, such as estate agents or stationery shops. Hotels may also be able to do this for you.

Airports now have Internet phones for use, with on-screen instructions. One of the most popular Portuguese websites, with information on anything and everything, from reviews to weather, shopping, news and useful information, is www.sapo.pt.

I'd like to...	Queria... *kree-uh...*
...send a fax	...mandar um fax *...man-dar oom*η *fax*
...use the Internet	...usar a Internet *...oo-sar uh Internet*
...send/receive an email	...mandar/receber um email *...man-dar/re-sse-bair oom*η *ee-mail*
...print a copy	...imprimir uma cópia *...im-pri-meer oo-muh co-pee-yuh*
How much does it cost?	Quanto custa? *kwan-too cush-tuh?*
How long does that give me?	Dá quanto tempo? *dah kwan-too tem-poo?*
I have a Hotmail account	Tenho uma conta Hotmail *tayn-yoo oo-muh con-tuh hotmail*

PROBLEMS

There seems to be a problem	Parece que há um problema *pa-<u>ress</u> kuh a oomη pro-<u>blay</u>-muh*
It won't connect	Não faz a ligação *nowη fash uh lee-ga-<u>ssown</u>*
It won't accept my name	Não aceita o meu nome *nowη a-<u>ssay</u>-tuh oo <u>may</u>-oo nom*
Is the server working?	O servidor está a funcionar? *oo ser-vee-<u>dor</u> shta uh fun-see-o-<u>nar</u>?*
Could you help me, please?	Podia ajudar-me, por favor? *po-<u>dee</u>-yuh a-zhoo-<u>dar</u>-muh, por fa-<u>vor</u>?*

BUSINESS LANGUAGE

The Portuguese are extremely formal when it comes to doing business, from the etiquette of clothes, to greetings and the way they address people. It is worth making note of this in order to impress.

People with a university degree are usually addressed as *senhor Doutor/senhora Doutora* (Doctor); those with a profession such as engineering or architecture may hear *senhor Doutor Engenheiro/senhora Doutora Arquitecta*, etc.

Business lunches may be quite extended affairs, with plenty of drink and cigarettes, although most working people eat in cafés and restaurants at lunchtime – it is relatively cheap, and it is rare for people to take their own packed lunch to work.

I'm...	Sou... *soh...*
...Mr (Brown)	...o senhor (Brown) *...oo sehn-<u>your</u> (Brown)*
...Mrs (Brown)	...a senhora (Brown) *...uh sehn-<u>your</u>-uh (Brown)*

...Miss (Brown)	...a senhora (Brown) *...uh sehn-your-uh (Brown)*
...(Charles Brown)	...o (Charles Brown) *...oo (Charles Brown)*
I'm from (Brown and Brown Ltd)	Sou de (Brown e Brown) Limitada *soh duh (Brown ee Brown) li-mee-ta-duh*
I have an appointment with...	Tenho um encontro marcado com... *tayn-yoo oomη en-con-troo mar-ka-doo comη...*
...the director	...o director/a directora *...oo di-reh-tor/uh di-reh-tor-uh*
...the manager	...o/a gerente *...oo/uh zheh-rent*
...the personnel manager	...o/a gerente de pessoal *...oo/uh zheh-rent duh peh-sso-al*
...the sales manager	...o/a gerente de vendas *...oo/uh zheh-rent duh ven-duhsh*
Could I...?	Poderia...? *po-duh-ree-yuh...?*
...see (speak to) Mr (Silva)	...falar com o senhor (Silva) *...fa-lar comη oo sehn-your (Silva)*
...speak to Mrs (Silva)	...falar com a senhora (Silva) *...fa-lar comη uh sehn-your-uh (Silva)*
Here is my card	Aqui está o meu cartão *a-key shta oo may-oo kar-townη*
I'm sorry I'm late	Desculpe o meu atraso *desh-koolp oo may-oo a-tra-soo*
I'm in the hotel (Central)	Estou no hotel (Central) *shtoh noo o-tel (sen-tral)*

I need...	Preciso... *pruh-<u>see</u>-soo...*
...a secretary	...duma secretária ...<u>doo</u>-muh se-kre-<u>tah</u>-ree-yuh
...an interpreter	...dum intérprete ...*doom in-<u>ter</u>-pret*
...a translator	...dum tradutor/duma tradutora ...*doom tra-doo-<u>tor</u>/<u>doo</u>-muh tra-doo-<u>tor</u>-uh*
Would you mind...?	Importava-se de...? *im-por-<u>tah</u>-vuh-suh duh...?*
...cancelling my appointment with	...cancelar o meu encontro com... ...*can-seh-<u>lar</u> oo <u>may</u>-oo en-<u>con</u>-troo comη...*
...making another appointment	...fazer outro encontro ...*fa-<u>zair</u> <u>oh</u>-troo en-<u>con</u>-troo*
...giving me some information about	...me dar informação sobre ...*me dar in-for-ma-<u>sown</u> <u>so</u>-bray*

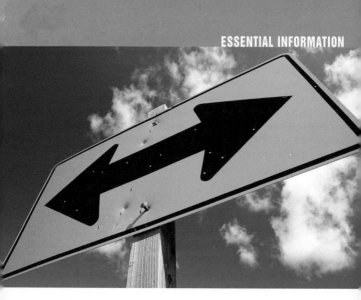

EMERGENCIES

POLICE

The emergency number is 112.

There are different police forces in Portugal, each with its own remit, including: the PSP (*Polícia de Segurança Pública* or Public Safety Police) are the main town centre force; the GNR (*Guarda Nacional Republicana* or National Guard) is military-based and controls law and order, particularly in rural areas; the *Brígada do Trânsito* (Traffic Brigade) is a division of the GNR, with red armbands; the *Guarda Fiscal* (Customs); *Polícia Marítima*; and *PJ* (*Polícia Judiciária*) (Criminal Investigation Unit).

The police, and their accompanying bureaucracy, are notoriously difficult to deal with in Portugal, so make sure you always have relevant documents to hand whilst driving, in case of accident or if you have to report a theft or assault.

If you find yourself in trouble with the police, you may be advised to seek the assistance of the nearest British Consulate.

Legal cases take an interminably long time to come to court, many as long as two to three years.

Portugal is still one of the safest countries to visit, with most crime being of the order of cheque fraud and theft. However, in Lisbon there has been an increase in drug-related attacks, so exercise caution.

Help!	Socorro! *soh-koh-roo!*
Thief!	Ladrão! *la-drown!*
Help me!	Ajude-me! *a-zhood-uh-muh!*
Stop!	Pare! *par!*
Fire!	Fogo! *foh-goo!*
Quick!	Depressa! *de-pray-ssuh!*
Call the police!	Chame a polícia! *sham uh po-lee-see-yuh!*
Where is the police station?	Onde fica a esquadra da polícia? *ond fee-kuh uh shkwa-druh duh po-lee-see-yuh?*
I'm lost	Estou perdido/a *shtoh per-dee-doo/uh*
My son/daughter is lost	O meu filho/a a minha filha está perdido/a *oo may-oo feel-yoo/uh meen-yuh feel-yuh shta per-dee-doo/uh*

My friend has disappeared	O meu amigo/a minha amiga desapareceu
	oo may-oo a-mee-goo/uh meen-yuh a-mee-guh des-a-pa-ruh-say-oo
Could you call the British Consulate?	Podia chamar ao Consulado Británico, por favor?
	po-dee-yuh sha-mar ow con-soo-la-doo bri-ta-nee-koo, por fa-vor?
I'd like to report a theft	Queria participar um roubo
	kree-uh par-ti-ssee-par oomη roh-boo
I've lost...	Perdi...
	per-dee...
Someone has stolen...	Roubaram-me...
	Roh-bah-rowη-muh...
...my camera	...a máquina fotográfica
	...uh ma-kee-nuh fo-toh-gra-fee-kuh
...my car	...o carro
	...oo kah-roo
...my car radio	...o rádio do carro
	...oo ra-dee-yoo doo kah-roo
...my jewels	...as jóias
	...uhsh zhoy-uhsh
...my luggage	...a bagagem
	...uh buh-ga-zhaymη
...my money	...o dinheiro
	...oo deen-yay-roo
...my purse	...o porta-moedas
	...oo por-tuh-moh-ay-duhsh
...my wallet	...a carteira
	...uh kar-tay-ruh

...my airline tickets	...os bilhetes de avião ...*oosh bil-yet-esh duh a-vee-yown*
...my (car) keys	...as chaves (do carro) ...*uhsh sha-vesh (doo kah-roo)*
...my driving licence	...a carta de condução ...*uh car-tuh duh con-doo ssown*
...my watch	...o relógio ...*oo re-loh-zhee-yoo*
...my passport	...o passaporte ...*oo pass-uh-port*
...my handbag	...a mala de mão ...*uh mal-uh duh mown*
It contained...	Continha... *con-tin-yuh...*
It has sentimental value	Tem valor sentimental *taymn va-lor sen-ti-men-tal*
I left it in the hotel/a taxi	Dexei-o no hotel/num táxi *day-shay-oo noo o-tel/noom tax-ee*
It happened...	Aconteceu... *a-con-tuh-say-oo...*
...a moment ago	...há um momento ...*ah oomn mo-men-too*
...this morning	...esta manhã ...*eh-shtuh muhn-yan*
...in the underground	...no metro ...*noo meh-troo*
...in the street	...na rua ...*nuh roo-uh*
It was a man/woman/child	Era um homem/uma mulher/uma criança *eh-ruh oomn om-emn/oo-muh mul-yair/oo-muh cree-yan-ssuh*

There was a gang of lads	Havia um grupo de moleques *ah-<u>vee</u>-yuh oomη <u>gru</u>-poo duh moh-<u>lek</u>-esh*
I don't know who	Não sei quem *nowη say kaymη*
I don't know...it happened	Não sei...aconteceu *nowη say...a-con-tuh-<u>say</u>-oo*
...when	...quando *...<u>kwan</u>-doo*
...where	...onde *...ond*
...how	...como *...<u>com</u>-oo*
It was an accident (not on purpose)	Foi sem querer *foy saymη kuh-<u>rair</u>*

DESCRIPTIONS

He/She is/was...	Ele/Ela é/era *el/<u>el</u>-uh eh/<u>eh</u>-ruh...*
...tall	...alto/a *...<u>al</u>-too/uh*
...short	...baixo/a *...<u>bye</u>-shoo/uh*
...medium height	...nem alto nem baixo *...naymη <u>al</u>-too naymη <u>bye</u>-shoo*
...fat	...gordo/a *...<u>gor</u>-doo/uh*
...thin	...magro/a *...<u>ma</u>-groo/uh*
...dark	...moreno/a *...moh-<u>ray</u>-noo/uh*

...blonde	...louro/a ..._loh_-roo/uh
...red-haired	...ruivo/a ...roo-_ee_-voo/uh
with...eyes	com olhos... comη _ol_-yoosh...
...blue	...azuis ...a-_zoo_-eesh
...green	...verdes ..._ver_-desh
...brown	...castanhos ...cash-_tan_-yoosh
...dark	...pretos ..._pray_-toosh
with...hair	com cabelo... comη ka-_beh_-loo...
...short	...curto ..._cur_-too
...long	...comprido ...com-_pree_-doo
...straight	...liso ..._lee_-ssoo
...curly	...encaracolado ...en-ka-rah-koh-_la_-doo
Bearded	Com barba comη _bar_-buh
With a moustache	Com bigode comη bee-_god_
(slightly) Bald	(um pouco) Careca (oomη _poh_-koo) ka-_re_-kuh
Wearing glasses	Com óculos comη _o_-koo-loosh

He/she is/was wearing...	Tem/Tinha... *taymη/<u>tin</u>-yuh...*
...a green shirt	...uma camisa verde *...<u>oo</u>-muh cam-<u>ee</u>-suh verd*
...white trousers	...calças brancas *...<u>kal</u>-ssuhsh <u>bran</u>-kuhsh*
...a blue dress	...um vestido azul *...oomη vesh-<u>tee</u>-doo a-<u>zool</u>*
...a big hat	...um chapéu grande *...oomη sha-<u>pay</u>-yoo grand*

You may hear:

Podia dar-me todos os detalhes? *po-<u>dee</u>-yuh <u>dar</u>-muh <u>toh</u>-doosh oosh day-<u>tal</u>-yuhsh?*	Could you give me all the details?
Como é? *<u>com</u>-oo eh?*	What is he/she/it like?
Quando...? *<u>kwan</u>-doo...?*	When...?
Onde...? *ond...?*	Where...?
Como...? *<u>com</u>-oo...?*	How...?
Quem...? *kaymη...?*	Who...?
...era? *...<u>eh</u>-ruh?*	...was it?
Não está cá *nowη shta ka*	He/She/It's not here
Avisaremos *a-vee-suh-<u>ray</u>-moosh*	We'll contact you/let you know
Precisa dum intérprete? *pruh-<u>see</u>-suh doom in-<u>ter</u>-pret?*	Do you need an interpreter?

Qual é o valor?
kwal eh oo va-lor?

What is its value?

O que continha?
oo kuh con-tin-yuh?

What did it contain?

Tem que preencher este impresso
*taymη kuh pray-en-shair esht
im-pray-ssoo*

You have to fill in this form

EMERGENCY TELEPHONE

112

ESSENTIAL INFORMATION

NUMBERS

0	Zero	*zeh-roo*
1	Um/Uma	*oomη/oo-muh*
2	Dois/Duas	*doysh/doo-uhsh*
3	Três	*traysh*
4	Quatro	*kwa-troo*
5	Cinco	*sin-koo*
6	Seis	*saysh*
7	Sete	*set*
8	Oito	*oy-too*
9	Nove	*nov*
10	Dez	*desh*
11	Onze	*onz*
12	Doze	*dohz*
13	Treze	*trez*
14	Catorze	*ka-torz*
15	Quinze	*kinz*

16	Dezasseis	*dehz-uh-<u>saysh</u>*
17	Dezassete	*dehz-uh-<u>set</u>*
18	Dezoito	*dehz-<u>oy</u>-too*
19	Dezanove	*dezh-uh-<u>nov</u>*
20	Vinte	*vint*
21	Vinte e um/uma	*vint ee oomη/<u>oo</u>-muh*
22	Vinte e dois/duas	*vint ee doysh/<u>doo</u>-uhsh*
30	Trinta	*<u>trin</u>-tuh*
40	Quarenta	*kwa-<u>ren</u>-tuh*
50	Cinquenta	*sin-<u>kwen</u>-tuh*
60	Sessenta	*se-<u>ssen</u>-tuh*
70	Setenta	*se-<u>ten</u>-tuh*
80	Oitenta	*oy-<u>ten</u>-tuh*
90	Noventa	*noh-<u>ven</u>-tuh*
100	Cem/cento	*saymη/<u>sen</u>-too*
101	Cento e um/uma	*<u>sen</u>-too ee oomη/<u>oo</u>-muh*
110	Cento e dez	*<u>sen</u>-too ee desh*
200	Duzentos/as	*doo-<u>zen</u>-toosh/(uhsh)*
300	Trezentos/as	*treh-<u>zen</u>-toosh/(uhsh)*
400	Quatrocentos/as	*kwa-troh-<u>ssen</u>-toosh/(uhsh)*
500	Quinhentos/as	*kin-<u>yen</u>-toosh/(uhsh)*
600	Seiscentos/as	*saysh-<u>sen</u>-toosh/(uhsh)*
700	Setecentos/as	*set-<u>ssen</u>-toosh/(uhsh)*
800	Oitocentos/as	*oy-too-<u>sen</u>-toosh/(uhsh)*
900	Novecentos/as	*nov-<u>sen</u>-toosh/(uhsh)*
1000	Mil	*mil*
2000	Dois mil	*doysh mil*

100 000	Cem mil	*saymη mil*
1 000 000	Um milhão	*oomη mil-yown*
2 000 000	Dois milhões	*doysh mil-yoηsh*

ORDINAL NUMBERS

First
Primeiro/a
pree-may-roo/uh

Second
Segundo/a
se-gun-doo/uh

Third
Terceiro/a
tair-say-roo/uh

Fourth
Quarto/a
kwar-too/uh

Fifth
Quinto/a
kin-too/uh

Sixth
Sexto/a
sesh-too/uh

Seventh
Sétimo/a
se-tee-moo/uh

Eighth
Oitavo/a
oy-tah-voo/uh

Ninth
Nono/a
noh-noo/uh

Tenth
Décimo/a
deh-ssee-moo/uh

Eleventh
Décimo primeiro/a
deh-ssee-moo pree-may-roo/uh

Twelfth
Décimo segundo
deh-ssee-moo se-gun-doo

Thirteenth
Décimo terceiro
deh-ssee-moo tair-say-roo

Fourteenth	Décimo quarto *deh-ssee-moo kwar-too*
Fifteenth	Décimo quinto *deh-ssee-moo kin-too*
Sixteenth	Décimo sexto *deh-ssee-moo sesh-too*
Seventeenth	Décimo sétimo *deh-ssee-moo se-tee-moo*
Eighteenth	Décimo oitavo *deh-ssee-moo oy-tah-voo*
Nineteenth	Décimo nono *deh-ssee-moo noh-noo*
Twentieth	Vigésimo *vee-zheh-see-moo*

MONTHS

Months	Os meses *oosh may-zesh*
January	Janeiro *zha-nay-roo*
February	Fevereiro *feh-vuh-ray-roo*
March	Março *mar-ssoo*
April	Abril *a-bril*
May	Maio *my-oo*
June	Junho *zhoon-yoo*
July	Julho *zhool-yoo*

August	Agosto *a-gosh-too*
September	Setembro *se-tem-broo*
October	Outubro *oh-too-broo*
November	Novembro *noh-vemŋ-broo*
December	Dezembro *deh-zem-broo*

SEASONS

Seasons	As estações *ush shta-ssoyŋsh*
Spring	A primavera *uh pree-muh-ve-ruh*
Summer	O verão *oo veh-rowŋ*
Autumn	O outono *oo oh-toh-noo*
Winter	O inverno *oo in-ver-noo*
In (the) summer	No verão *noo veh-rowŋ*
Every winter	Todos os invernos/cada inverno *toh-doosh oosh in-ver-noosh/cah-duh in-ver-noo*

DAYS

| Days of the week | Os dias da semana
oosh dee-yuhsh duh suh-mah-nuh |
| Monday | Segunda-feira*
se-gun-duh-fay-ruh |

Tuesday	Terça-feira*
	tair-ssuh-_fay_-ruh
Wednesday	Quarta-feira*
	kwar-tuh-_fay_-ruh
Thursday	Quinta-feira*
	kin-tuh-_fay_-ruh
Friday	Sexta-feira*
	sesh-tuh-_fay_-ruh
Saturday	Sábado
	_sa_-ba-doo
Sunday	Domingo
	doh-_min_-goo

* in colloquial speech, _feira_ is often dropped

DATES

In July	Em Julho
	aymη _zhool_-yoo
What's the date today?	Que dia é hoje?
	kuh _dee_-yuh eh ozh?
It's...	É...
	eh...
...the 1st of August	...o dia um de Agosto
	...oo _dee_-yuh oomη dee a-_gosh_-too
...the 10th of May	...o (dia) dez de Maio
	...oo (_dee_-yuh) desh duh _my_-oo
Weekend	O fim da semana
	oo fimη duh se-_man_-uh
Working days	Os dias da semana
	oosh _dee_-yuhsh duh se-_man_-uh
On Monday	Na segunda (-feira)
	nuh se-_gun_-duh (-_fay_-ruh)

On Saturdays	Aos sábados
	owsh sa-ba-doosh
Every Thursday	Todas as quintas/cada quinta (-feira)
	toh-duhsh uhsh kin-tuhsh/cah-duh kin-tuh (-fay-ruh)

TIME

What time is it?	Que horas são?
	kay or-uhsh sown?
It's one o'clock	É uma hora
	eh oo-muh or-uh
It's two o'clock	São duas horas
	sown doo-uhsh or-uhsh
It's five past three	São três e cinco
	sown traysh ee sin-koo
It's twenty past six	São seis e vinte
	sown saysh ee vint
It's a quarter past eight	São oito e um quarto/e quinze
	sown oy-too ee oomη kwar-too/ee kinz
It's half past ten	São dez e meia
	sown desh ee may-uh
It's ten to five	São cinco menos dez
	sown sin-koo may-noosh desh
It's a quarter to seven	São sete menos um quarto/quinze
	sown set may-noosh oomη kwar-too/kinz
...am	...de manhã
	...duh muhn-yaη
...pm (afternoon/early evening)	...de tarde
	...duh tard
...pm (night)	...à noite
	...a noyt

Midday	Meio-dia _may_-oo–_dee_-yuh
Midnight	Meia-noite _may_-uh noyt
At what time...?	A que horas...? uh kay _or_-uhsh...?
At nine o'clock	Às nove (horas) azh nov (_or_-uhsh)
From six until seven	Das seis (até) às sete duhsh saysh (uh-_tay_) azh set
From ten o'clock (onwards)	A partir das dez Uh par-_teer_ duhsh desh
In ten minutes	Daqui a dez minutos Duh-_key_ uh desh mee-_noo_-toosh
An hour ago	Há uma hora Ah _oo_-muh _or_-uh
Today	Hoje ozh
Yesterday	Ontem _on_-taymŋ
Tomorrow	Amanhã uh-muhn-_yaŋ_
In the morning	De manhã duh muhn-_yaŋ_
In the afternoon/evening	De tarde duh tard
At night	À noite a noyt
Last night	Ontem à noite _on_-taymŋ a noyt
This morning	Hoje de manhã/esta manhã ozh duh muhn-_yaŋ_/_eh_-shtuh muhn-_yaŋ_

This afternoon/evening	Hoje à tarde/noite *ozh a tard/noyt*
Tonight	Esta noite *<u>eh</u>-shtuh noyt*
The day before yesterday	Anteontem *an-tee-<u>on</u>-taymη*
The day after tomorrow	Depois de amanhã *de-<u>poysh</u> duh uh-muhn-<u>yaη</u>*
Next week	A semana próxima *uh suh-<u>mah</u>-nuh <u>pro</u>-ssee-muh*
Next Tuesday	A terça (-feira) próxima *uh <u>tair</u>-ssuh (-<u>fay</u>-ruh) <u>pro</u>-ssee-muh*
Last Wednesday	A quarta (-feira) passada *uh <u>kwar</u>-tuh (-<u>fay</u>-ruh) puh-<u>ssah</u>-duh*
Before	Antes *<u>an</u>-tush*
After	Depois *de-<u>poysh</u>*
Until	Até *uh-<u>tay</u>*
During	Durante *doo-<u>rant</u>*
At the beginning	Ao princípio *ow prin-<u>ssip</u>-yoo*
In the middle	No meio *noo <u>may</u>-oo*
At the end	Ao fim *ow feemη*

PUBLIC HOLIDAYS

When a bank holiday falls on either a Thursday or a Tuesday, the Portuguese, like the French, do what is called *fazer a ponte* (make the bridge). That is, they also take off the intervening day as extra holiday!

The Portuguese traditionally spend as much of their holiday time as possible with their family, either at home, visiting relatives, or at the seaside.

Bank holidays commemorating special events are generally marked with public celebrations, parades, and street parties. Even the smallest town or village has a number of its own feast days throughout the year.

1 January	New Year	Ano Novo
Feb/March	Carnival	Carnaval
March/April	Easter	Páscoa
25 April	Liberty Day	Dia da Liberdade
1 May	Labour Day	Dia do Trabalhador
June	Corpus Christi	Corpo de Deus
10 June	Portugal Day	O Dia de Portugal
13 June (Lisbon)	St Anthony's Day	Santo António
24 June (Porto)	St John's Day	São João
15 August	Assumption Day	Assunção de Nossa Senhora
5 October	Republic Day	Implantação da República
1 November	All Saints' Day	Dia de Todos os Santos
1 December	Restoration of Independence	Restauração da Independência
8 December	Immaculate Conception	Imaculada Conceição
25 December	Christmas	Natal

OTHER IMPORTANT FESTIVALS

New Year's Eve	A Passagem do Ano
6 January Epiphany – Kings' Day	O Dia dos Reis
Shrove Tuesday	Terça-feira Gorda
Ash Wednesday	Quarta-feira de Cinzas
Lent	Quaresma
Holy Week	Semana Santa
Good Friday	Sexta-feira Santa
Easter Sunday	Domingo de Páscoa
All Souls' Day	O Dia dos Defuntos
Christmas Eve	A Véspera de Natal

DICTIONARY

Both masculine and feminine forms are given for adjectives
e.g. allergic: alérgico/a=alérgico (m)/alérgica (f).
f indicates a feminine noun; m indicates a masculine noun.
Translating 'a' and 'the' in Portuguese depends on whether the words
you are using are masculine or feminine, and singular or plural.

	Masc. Sing.	Fem. Sing.	Masc. Plur.	Fem. Plur.
a/an/some	um	uma	uns	umas
the	o	a	os	as

A
a um, uma
abdomen abdômen (m)
able: to be able poder
about sobre, cerca, mais ou menos
above em cima (de)
abroad ao estrangeiro
abscess abcesso (m)
accelerator acelerador (m)
to accept aceitar
accident acidente (m)
accommodation alojamento (m)
account conta (f)
ache dor (f)
across através/ao outro lado
activity actividade (f)
actor actor (m)
actress actriz (f)
adaptor adaptor (m)
address morada (f)
adhesive tape fita adesiva (f)
admission charge preço de entrada (m)
to admit admitir
adult adulto (m)
advance (cash) adiantamento (m)
advertisement anúncio (m)
aerial antena (f)
aeroplane avião (m)
after depois (de)

afternoon tarde (f)
aftershave loção para a barba (f)
again outra vez
against contra
age idade (f)
agent agente/representante (m/f)
to agree concordar
air ar (m)
air conditioning ar condicionado (m)
air freshener desodorizante de
  ambiente (m)
air hostess hospedeira do ar (f)
airline linha aérea (f)
airmail via aérea (f)
airport aeroporto (m)
alarm clock despertador (m)
alcohol álcool (m)
all todo/a/os/as, tudo
  that's all é tudo
allergic alérgico/a
almost quase
alone só; sozinho/a
already já
also também
although embora
always sempre
amazing incrível
ambulance ambulância (f)
America os Estados Unidos

American americano/a
amount quantidade (f)
amusing divertido/a
anaesthetic anestésico (m)
and e
angry zangado/a
animal animal (m)
ankle tornozelo (m)
annoyed irritado/a
anorak anorak (m)
another outro/a
answer resposta (f)
answering machine atendedor
  automático (m)
antibiotic antibiótico (m)
antidote antídoto (m)
antifreeze anticongelante (m)
antique antiguidade (f)
antiseptic antiséptico (m)
anxious preocupado/a
any algum/a, nenhum/a
anything alguma coisa (f)
apartment apartamento (m)
apology desculpas (fpl)
appendicitis apendicite (m)
appetite apetite (m)
apple maçã (f)
application form ficha de inscrição (f)
appointment consulta (f)/encontro
  marcado (m)
approximately aproximadamente
apricot damasco (m)
architect arquitecto/a (m/f)
area área (f)
area code indicativo (m)
arm braço (m)
armchair poltrona (f)
around ao redor (de)
arrival chegada (f)
to arrive chegar
art arte (f)
art gallery galeria de arte (f)
artichoke alcachofra (f)
artist artista (m/f)
ashtray cinzeiro (m)
to ask perguntar
to ask for pedir
asleep adormecido/a; a dormir
asparagus espargo (m)

aspirin aspirina (f)
assistant assistente/auxiliar (m/f)
asthma asma (f)
at a/em
atmosphere ambiente (m)
attack ataque (m)
attention atenção (f)
attic sótão (m)
attractive atraente
aubergine beringela (f)
aunt tia (f)
Australia a Austrália
Australian australiano/a
automatic automático/a
autumn outono (m)
avocado abacate (m)
away (far off) longe
  go away! vá-se embora!
awful horrível
axle eixo (m)

B
baby bebé (m)
babysitter baby-sitter (m/f)
back para trás
  (body) costas (fpl)
backache dor das costas (f)
bacon toucinho/bacon (m)
bad mau/má
bag saco (m); mala de mão (f)
baggage bagagem (f)
bakery padaria (f)
balcony varanda (f)
ball (dance) baile (m)
  (toy) bola (f)
ballpoint pen esferográfica (f)
ban proibição (f)
  to ban proibir
banana banana (f)
band grupo (m); orquestra (f)
bandage ligadura (f)
bank banco (m)
bank holiday feriado (m)
banknote nota (f)
bar bar (m)
barbecue churrasco (m)
barber's shop barbeiro (m)
bargain pechincha (f)
basement cave (f)

basin lavatório (m)
basket cesta (f)
basketball basquete (m)
bath banheira (f)
  to bathe banhar-se; tomar banho
bathing cap touca (f)
bathrobe roupão de banho (m)
bathroom casa de banho (f)
battery (car) bateria (f)
  (torch etc) pilha (f)
bay bahia (f)
to be ser; estar
beach praia (f)
bean feijão (m); fava (f)
beard barba (f)
beautiful bonito/a
beauty salon salão de beleza (m)
because porque
bed cama (f)
bedding roupa de cama (f)
bedroom quarto (m)
bee abelha (f)
beef carne de vaca (f)
beer cerveja (f)
beetroot beterraba (f)
before antes (de)
to begin começar
beginner principiante (m/f)
behind atrás
beige bege
bell campainha (f)
below abaixo/debaixo de
belt cinto (m)
bench banco (m)
bend (in road) curva (f)
best o/a melhor
better melhor
between entre
bib babadouro (m)
bicycle bicicleta (f)
big grande
bikini biquini (m)
bill conta (f)
bin caixote do lixo (m)
bin liner saco de lixo (m)
binoculars binóculo (m)
bird pássaro (m)
birthday dia de anos (m)
biscuit bolacha (f); biscoito (m)

bite mordida; picada (f)
  to bite morder; picar
bitter amargo/a
black preto/a
blackberry amora (f)
blanket cobertor (m)
bleach lexivia (f)
bleeding sangue (m)
blind (window) persiana (f)
blind (see) cego/a
blister bolha (f)
blonde louro/a
blood sangue (m)
blood pressure tensão arterial (m)
blouse blusa (f)
blue azul
boat barco (m)
body corpo (m)
boil furúnculo (m)
  to boil ferver
boiled cozido/a
boiled egg ovo cozido (m)
to bolt trancar
bone osso (m)
  (fish) espinha (f)
book livro (m)
  to book reservar
booking office bilheteira (f)
bookshop livraria (f)
boot (shoe) bota (f)
  (car) boot porta bagagens (m)
border fronteira (f)
boring aborrecido/a; chato/a
both ambos/as
bottle garrafa (f)
bottle-opener abre-garrafas (m)
bottom (depth) fundo (m)
bowl tigela (f)
box caixa (f)
box office bilheteira (f)
boy rapaz (m)
boyfriend namorado (m)
bra soutien (m)
bracelet pulseira (f)
brake fluid líquido de travões (m)
brakes travões (mpl)
brand marca (f)
brandy conhaque (m)
bread pão (m)

to break partir
breakdown (car) avaria (f)
breakdown lorry pronto socorro (m)
breakfast pequeno almoço (m)
breast peito (m)
 to breathe respirar
bridge ponte (f)
briefcase pasta (f)
to bring trazer
Britain a Grã Bretanha
British britânico/a
brochure folheto (m)
broken partido/a; estragado/a
broom vassoura (f)
brother irmão (m)
brown castanho/a
bruise nódoa negra (f)
brush escova (f)
bucket balde (m)
building edifício (m)
bulb lâmpada (f)
bull touro (m)
bullfight tourada; corrida de touros (f)
bullring praça de touros (f)
to bump bater
bumper pára-choques (m)
bunch (flowers) ramo (m)
bungalow bangaló (m)
bunk beliche (m)
burglar ladrão; gatuno (m)
burglary assalto (m)
burn queimadura (f)
 to burn queimar
bus autocarro (m)
business negócio (m)
business trip viagem de negócios (f)
bus station estação de autocarros (f); terminal (m)
bus stop paragem de autocarro (f)
busy ocupado/a; movimentado/a
but mas
butcher's talho (m)
butter manteiga (f)
button botão (m)
 to buy comprar

C
cab táxi (m)
cabbage couve (f)

cable car teleférico (m)
cable TV TV por cabo (f)
café café (m)
cake bolo (m)
cake shop pastelaria (f)
calendar calendário (m)
call chamada (f)
 to call (shout/telephone) chamar
camera máquina fotográfica (f)
camp parque de campismo (m)
to camp acampar
can (to be able) poder
can lata (f)
Canada o Canadá
Canadian canadense (m/f)
canal canal (m)
to cancel cancelar; anular
candle vela (f)
candy rebuçado (m)
can opener abre-latas (m)
car automóvel; carro (m)
caravan rulotte (m); caravana (f)
carburettor carburador (m)
card (visiting) cartão (m)
 postcard postal (m)
 membership carnet (m)
cardigan casaco (de lã) (m)
careful! cuidado!
car hire aluguel de automóveis (m)
car park parque de estacionamento (m)
carpet tapete (m)
carriage carruagem (f); vagão (m)
carrot cenoura (f)
to carry levar
carrycot porta-bebé (m)
carton caixa (de papelão) (f)
car wash lavagem automática (f)
case (for glasses etc) estojo (m)
 (suitcase) mala (f)
cash dinheiro (m)
 to cash levantar; trocar
cash desk caixa (f)
cashier caixa (m/f)
cassette cassette (f)
castle castelo (m)
cat gato (m)
cathedral catedral; sé (f)
cauliflower couve-flor (f)
cave gruta (f)

celery aipo (m)
cellar adega; cave (f)
central heating aquecimento central (m)
centre centro (m)
century século (m)
ceramics cerámica (f)
certificate certificado (m)
chain cadeia; rede (f)
chair cadeira (f)
chalet chalé (m)
champagne champanhe (m)
change troco (m)
to change trocar; mudar
changing room gabinete de provas (m)
chapel capela (f)
to charge cobrar
charter flight voo charter (m)
cheap barato/a
to check verificar; ver
to check in fazer o check-in
cheerio! até logo!; tchau!
cheers! saúde!
cheese queijo (m)
chemist's farmácia (f)
cheque cheque (m)
chequebook talão de cheques (m)
cheque card cartão de cheques (m)
cherry cereja (f)
chest peito (m)
chewing gum pastilha elástica (f)
chicken galinha (f); frango (m)
child criança (f)
children crianças (fpl)
china porcelana (f)
chips batatas fritas (fpl)
chlorine cloro (m)
chocolate chocolate (m)
chop costeleta (f)
Christmas Natal (m)
church igreja (f)
cider sidra (f)
cigar charuto (m)
cigarette cigarro (m)
cigarette lighter isqueiro (m)
cinema cinema (m)
circle (theatre) balcão (m)
circus circo (m)
city cidade (f)
city centre centro da cidade (m)

civil servant funcionário/a público/a
claim reclamação (f)
to claim reclamar
class classe (f)
clean limpo/a
to clean limpar
clear claro/a
client cliente (m/f)
climate clima (m)
clinic clínica (f)
cloakroom vestiário (m)
clock relógio (m)
close (near) perto/a
(stuffy) abafado/a
to close fechar; encerrar
closed fechado/a
cloth tecido (m)
clothes roupa (f)
cloud nuvem (f)
club clube (m)
clutch (car) embraiagem (f)
coach camioneta (f)
coast costa (f)
coat casaco (m)
coat hanger cabide (m)
cocoa cacau (m)
coconut coco (m)
code código (m)
coffee café (m)
coin moeda (f)
cold frio/a
to be cold (person) ter frio
(weather) estar/fazer frio
to have a cold estar constipado/a
collar gola (f)
colour cor (f)
comb pente (m)
to come vir
comedy comédia (f)
comfortable confortável
comic (magazine) revista de banda;
desenhada (f)
compact disc CD (m)
company companhia; empresa (f)
to complain queixar-se
complaint queixa (f)
complicated complicado/a
computer computador (m)
concert concerto (m)

concussion concussão cerebral (f)
conditioner creme amaciador (m)
condom preservativo (m)
conductor (bus) cobrador/a
confectioner's confeitaria (f)
congratulations parabéns!
connection (transport) ligação (f)
constipated com prisão de ventre
consulate consulado (m)
contact lens lente de contacto (f)
contagious contagioso/a
contraceptive (pill) (pílula)
  anticoncepcional (f)
control controle (m)
controller controlador/a (m/f)
cook cozinheiro/a (m/f)
  to cook cozinhar
cooker fogão (m)
cooking utensils utensílios de cozinha
  (mpl)
cool fresco/a
cork rolha (f)
corkscrew saca-rolhas (m)
corn trigo; milho (m)
corner esquina (f)
corridor corredor (m)
cosmetics cosméticos (mpl)
cost preço (m)
  to cost custar
costume traje (m)
cot cama de bebé (f)
cottage casa de campo (f)
cottage cheese queijo fresco;
  requeijão (m)
cotton algodão (m)
cotton wool algodão hidrófilo (m)
cough tosse (f)
  to cough tossir
counter (shop) balcão (m)
country país (m)
countryside campo (m)
couple casal (m)
courgette courgette (m)
course (meal) prato (m)
  (golf) campo (m)
cousin primo/a (m/f)
crab caranguejo (m)
crafts artesanato (m)
cramp cãibra (f)

crash batida (f)
crash course curso intensivo (m)
crash helmet capacete (m)
cream natas (fpl); creme (m)
credit card cartão de crédito (m)
crisps batatinhas fritas (fpl)
crossing passadeira (f)
crossroads cruzamento (m)
crowded apinhado/a
cruise cruzeiro (m)
cucumber pepino (m)
cuisine cozinha (f)
cup chávena (f)
cupboard armário (m)
to cure curar
currency moeda (f)
current corrente
curtain cortina (f)
cushion almofada (f)
custard creme (m)
customer cliente (m/f)
customs alfândega (f)
to cut cortar
cutlery talheres (mpl)
cycling ciclismo (m)
cyclist ciclista (m/f)

D
daily diariamente
dairy leitaria (f)
damp húmido/a
dance baile (m)
  to dance dançar
dance hall sala de festas (f)
danger perigo (m)
dangerous perigoso/a
dark escuro/a
date (calendar) data (f)
  (fruit) tâmara (f)
daughter filha (f)
day dia (m)
dead morto/a
deaf surdo/a
dear caro/a
  Dear Sir/Madam (letter) estimado/a
  senhor/a
deck chair cadeira de lona (f);
  espreguiçadeira (f)
deep fundo/a

to dehydrate desidratar
delay atraso (m)
delicate delicado/a; frágil
delicatessen charcutaria (f)
delivery service serviço a domicílio (m)
dentist dentista (m/f)
denture dentadura (f)
deodorant desodorizante (m)
department departamento (m)
department store grande armazém (m)
departure partida (f)
deposit depósito; sinal (m)
  to deposit (bank) depositar
dessert sobremesa (f)
detergent detergente (m)
detour desvio (m)
to develop (film) revelar
diabetes diabete (f)
diabetic diabético/a
to dial marcar
dialling tone sinal de marcar (m)
diarrhoea diarreia (f)
dictionary dicionário (m)
diesel gasóleo (m)
diet dieta (f)
different diferente
difficult difícil
dining-car vagão restaurante (m)
dining-room sala de jantar (f)
dinner jantar (m)
dinner jacket smoking (m)
direct directo/a
direction direcção (f)
directory lista (telefónica) (f)
dirty sujo/a
disabled deficiente; inválido/a
discount desconto (m)
dish prato (m)
dishwasher máquina de lavar louça (f)
disinfectant desinfectante (m)
distance distância (f)
to disturb incomodar
diversion desvio (m)
divorced divorciado/a
dizzy tonto/a
doctor médico/a (m/f)
document documento (m)
dog cão (m)
doll boneca (f)

dollar dólar (m)
door porta (f)
doorbell campaínha (f)
double duplo/a
double bed cama de casal (f)
double room quarto de casal (m)
down em baixo
downstairs em baixo
dozen dúzia (f)
drawer gaveta (f)
dress vestido (m)
drier secador (m)
drink bebida (f)
  to drink beber
drinking water água potável (f)
to drive conduzir
driving licence carta de condução (f)
drug remédio; medicamento (m)
drugs drogas (fpl)
drunk bêbado/a
dry seco/a
to dry-clean limpar a seco
dry-cleaner's limpeza a seco (f)
dummy (baby) chupeta (f)
during durante
dustbin caixote de lixo (m)
duster pano de pó (m)
duty (tax) imposto (m)
duty-free duty-free (m)

E
each cada
ear orelha (f); ouvido (m)
earache dor (f) de ouvidos
early cedo
earring brinco (m)
east (l)este (m)
easy fácil
to eat comer
eczema eczema (m)
egg ovo (m)
either qualquer
elastic elástico/a
elbow cotovelo (m)
electric eléctrico/a
electrician electricista (m/f)
electricity electricidade (f)
email correio electrónico (m)
embassy embaixada (f)

emergency emergência (f)
emergency cord sinal de alarme (m)
emergency exit saída de emergência (f)
employer empregador/a (m/f)
empty vazio/a
end fim (m)
engaged ocupado/a
engine motor (m)
England a Inglaterra
English inglês/inglesa
to enjoy oneself divertir-se
enjoyable agradável
enough suficiente
to enrol (school) inscrever-se;
  matricular-se
entertaining divertido/a
entrance entrada (f)
envelope envelope (m)
environment ambiente (m)
epilepsy epilepsia (f)
equipment equipamento (m)
error erro (m)
escalator escada rolante (f)
evening (early) tarde (f)
  (late) noite (f)
every cada
everyone toda a gente (f); todos (mpl)
everything tudo
everywhere por toda a parte
exactly exactamente
excellent excelente
exchange rate câmbio (m)
excursion excursão (f)
excuse me! desculpe!
exercise exercício (m)
exhaust pipe tubo de escape (m)
exhibition exposição (f)
exit saída (f)
expenses despesas (fpl)
expensive caro/a
to export exportar
express (delivery) urgente
  (train) comboio rápido (m)
extension (telephone) extensão (f)
eye olho (m)
eye drops gotas para os olhos (f)
eye shadow sombra (f)
eye specialist oftalmologista (m/f)
eye witness testemunha (f)

F
fabric tecido (m)
face cara (f)
factory fábrica (f)
to faint desmaiar
fair (hair) louro/a
  (funfair) feira (f)
  (just) justo/a
fall queda (f)
  to fall cair
family família (f)
fan (hand) leque (m)
  (electric) ventoínha (f)
  (sports) fan (m/f)
fan belt correia da ventoínha (f)
fantastic fantástico/a
far longe
fare preço (da passagem) (m)
farm quinta (f)
fashion moda (f)
fast rápido/a
to fasten fechar
fat (meat) gordura (f)
  (person) gordo/a
father pai (m)
fault (person) culpa (f)
  (object) defeito (m)
fax fax (m)
fee preço (m)
feeding bottle mamadeira (f)
to feel (ill) sentir-se (mal)
  (touch) tocar
ferry barco de travessia/ferry-boat (m)
fever febre (f)
few poucos/as
fiancé noivo (m)
fiancée noiva (f)
field campo (m)
fig figo (m)
to fill encher
filling (tooth) chumbo (m)
filling station posto de gasolina (m)
film (cinema) filme (m)
  (photo) rolo de filme (m)
filter filtro (m)
fine! está bem!
finger dedo (m)
to finish terminar
fire fogueira (f); incêndio (m)
  (gas or electric) aquecedor (m)

fire alarm alarme de incêndio (m)
fire brigade bombeiros (mpl)
fire escape escada de emergência (f)
fire extinguisher extintor (m)
fireplace lareira (f)
fireproof incombustível
firm (business) empresa (f)
first primeiro/a
first aid primeiros socorros (mpl)
first floor primeiro andar (m)
first name nome próprio (m)
fish peixe (m)
 to fish pescar
fishbone espinha (f)
fishing rod cana de pesca (f)
fishmonger's peixaria (f)
fitting room gabinete de prova (f)
fizzy com gás
flag bandeira (f)
flashlight lanterna de bolsa (f)
flat plano/a
 (battery) descarregado/a
 (apartment) apartamento (m)
flat tyre pneu furado (m)
flavour sabor (m)
flea pulga (f)
flight voo (m)
flip-flops chinelas (fpl)
flippers barbatanas (fpl)
floor (ground) chão (m)
 (in building) andar (m)
florist's florista (f)
flour farinha (f)
flower flor (f)
flu gripe (f)
fly mosca (f)
 to fly voar
fog nevoeiro (m)
folding dobrável
food comida (f)
food poisoning intoxicação alimentar (f)
foot pé (m)
football futebol (m)
footpath caminho (m)
for por/para
forbidden proibido/a
forecast (weather) previsão (f)
forehead testa (f)
foreigner estrangeiro/a (m/f)
forest floresta (f)

fork garfo (m)
form (shape) forma (f)
 (document) ficha (f); impresso (m)
fortnight quinzena (f); quinze dias
fountain fonte (f)
fourth quarto/a
fracture fractura (f)
fragile frágil
free (vacant) livre
 (no charge) gratuito/a
freezer congelador (m)
frequent frequente
fresh fresco/a
fridge frigorífico (m)
fried frito/a
friend amigo/a (m/f)
friendly simpático/a
from de/desde
front da frente
frontier fronteira (f)
frozen congelado/a
fruit fruta (f)
fruit juice sumo de fruta (m)
fruit salad salada de frutas (f)
 to fry fritar
frying pan frigideira (f)
full cheio/a
full board pensão completa (f)
funny (comic) engraçado/a
 (strange) estranho/a
furnished mobilado/a
furniture móveis (mpl)
further mais longe
fuse fusível (m)
fuse box caixa de fusíveis (f)

G
game jogo (m)
garage garagem (f)
garden jardim (m)
garlic alho (m)
gas gás (m)
gate portão (m)
gay homosexual
gear (car) velocidade (f)
gearbox caixa de velocidades (f)
general geral
gentleman senhor; cavalheiro (m)
gents senhores/WC
 to get obter; ir buscar

to get up levantar-se
gift prenda (f); presente (m)
gin gin (m)
ginger gengibre (m)
girl rapariga (f)
girlfriend namorada (f)
to give dar
glad feliz; contente
glass copo (m)
glasses óculos (mpl)
glove luva (f)
glue cola (f)
to go ir
 to go out sair
gold ouro (m)
golf golfe (m)
golf club (group) clube de golfe (m)
 (stick) taco de golfe (m)
golf course campo de golfe (m)
good bom/boa
good afternoon boa tarde
goodbye adeus
good evening boa tarde/noite
good morning bom dia
good night boa noite
goods artigos (mpl)
government governo (m)
gram grama (m)
grandchild neto/a (m/f)
grandfather avô (m)
grandmother avó (f)
grandparents avós (mpl)
grape uva (f)
grapefruit toranja (f)
grass relva (f)
gravy molho (de carne) (m)
greasy gordurento/a
Great Britain a Grã-Bretanha
green verde
greengrocer's frutaria (f)
greetings cumprimentos (mpl);
 felicitações (fpl)
grey cinzento/a
grill grelha (f)
grilled grelhado/a
grocer's mercearia (f)
ground chão (m)
ground floor rés-do-chão (m)
groundsheet capa impermeável (f)

group grupo (m)
guarantee garantia (f)
guard guarda (m)
guest convidado/a; hóspede (m/f)
guest-house pensão (f)
guide guia (m/f)
guidebook guia (m)
guided tour excursão guiada (f)
guitar guitarra (f)/viola (f)
gum (teeth) gengiva (f)
 (chewing) pastilha elástica (f)
gun espingarda; pistola (f)

H
hair cabelo/s (m/mpl)
hairbrush escova de cabelo (f)
hairdresser's cabeleireiro (m)
hair dryer secador de cabelo (m)
hairspray laca para o cabelo (m)
half metade (f); meio/a
half board meia-pensão (f)
ham fiambre (m)
hamburger hamburger (m)
hammer martelo (m)
hand mão (f)
handbag mala (de mão) (f)
handbrake travão de mão (m)
handkerchief lenço (m)
handle (door) maçaneta (f)
handmade feito/a a mão
hanger cabide (m)
hangover ressaca (f)
happy feliz
harbour porto (m)
hard duro/a
hard-boiled egg ovo cozido (m)
hat chapéu (m)
to have ter
hay fever febre dos fenos (f)
head cabeça (f)
headache dor de cabeça (f)
headlights faróis (mpl)
health saúde (f)
healthy saudável
to hear ouvir
hearing aid aparelho auditivo (m)
heart coração (m)
heart attack ataque cardíaco (m)
heat calor (m)

heater aquecedor (m)
heating aquecimento (m)
heavy pesado/a
heel (shoe) salto (m)
 (body) calcanhar (m)
hello! olá!
help! socorro!
help ajuda (f)
 to help ajudar
here aqui; cá
hi-fi aparelhagem de som (f)
high alto/a
high-chair cadeira de bebé (f)
high street rua principal (f)
to hire alugar
to hitch-hike pedir boleia
hole buraco (m)
holiday (national) feriado (m)
holiday resort estância de turismo (f)
holidays férias (fpl)
home casa (f)
home address morada (f)
honey mel (m)
honeymoon lua de mel (f)
horn (car) buzina (f)
horrible horrível
horse cavalo (m)
horse-riding andar a cavalo (m)
hospital hospital (m)
hostel (youth) pousada de juventude (f)
hot quente
 to be hot (person) ter calor
 (weather) fazer calor
hotel hotel (m)
hour hora (f)
house casa (f)
housewife dona de casa (f)
how? como?
how big? de que tamanho?
how far? a que distância?
how long? quanto tempo?
how much? quanto?
humid húmido/a
to be hungry ter fome
to be in a hurry ter/estar com pressa
hurry up! de pressa!
to hurt doer; magoar
husband marido (m)

I

ice gelo (m)
ice cream gelado (m)
ice cube cubo de gelo (m)
ice lolly gelado (m)
idea ideia (f)
identity card cartão de identidade (m)
ignition ignição (f)
ill doente
illegal ilegal
illness doença (f)
immediately imediatamente
to import importar
important importante
impossible impossível
in em; dentro
included incluído/a
indicator indicador (m)
indigestion indigestão (f)
indoor interior
indoor pool piscina coberta (f)
industry indústria (f)
infection infecção (f)
infectious contagioso/a
information informação (f)
inhaler inalador (m)
injection injecção (f)
injury ferida (f)
inn estalagem (f)
inquiries informações (fpl)
insect bite picada de insecto (f)
inside dentro
insurance seguro (m)
insurance company companhia de
 seguros (f)
interesting interessante
international internacional
internet internet (f)
interpreter intérprete (m/f)
intersection cruzamento (m)
interval intervalo (m)
to invest investir
invitation convite (m)
to invite convidar
invoice factura (f)
Ireland a Irlanda
Irish irlandês/irlandesa
iron (utensil) ferro (de passar roupa) (m)
 (metal) ferro (m)

to iron passar roupa
ironmonger ferreiro (m)
island ilha (f)
itch comichão (f)
itinerary itinerário (m)

J

jacket casaco (curto) (m)
jail prisão; cadeia (f)
jam doce (m); geleia (f)
jar jarro; pote; frasco (m)
jeans calças de ganga (fpl); jeans (mpl)
jellyfish alforreca (f)
jersey camisola (f)
jewellery jóias (fpl)
job emprego (m)
to go jogging ir correr
journey viagem (f)
juice sumo (m)
jumper camisola (f)
junction cruzamento (m)

K

to keep guardar
kettle chaleira (f)
key chave (f)
kidney rim (m)
kilo quilo (m)
kilometre quilómetro (m)
kind (nice) simpático/a
 (type) tipo (m)
kitchen cozinha (f)
knee joelho (m)
knickers cuecas (fpl)
knife faca (f)
to knock (on door) bater (à porta)
to know (facts) saber
 (people/places) conhecer

L

label etiqueta (f)
lace (shoe) atacador (m)
 (fabric) renda (f)
ladder escada de mão (f)
ladies (toilets) senhoras/WC
lady senhora (f)
lager cerveja (f)
lake lago (m)

lamb cordeiro (m)
lamp (table) lâmpada (f)
 (street) poste de iluminação (m)
land terra (f)
landscape paisagem (f)
lane (country) caminho (m)
 (motorway) faixa (f)
language língua (f)
large grande
last último/a
last night ontem à noite
late (time) tarde
 (delayed) atrasado/a
later mais tarde
launderette lavandaria (f)
lavatory casa de banho (f); sanitários (mpl)
law lei (f)
lawyer advogado/a (m/f)
laxative laxativo (m)
lead (metal) chumbo (m)
leaflet folheto (m)
leak goteira (f); furo (m)
 to leak gotejar; vazar
lean (meat) magro/a
to learn aprender
leather pele (f); cabedal; couro (m)
to leave (depart) partir
left esquerda (f)
left luggage depósito de bagagens (m)
leftovers restos (mpl)
leg perna (f)
leisure lazer (m)
lemon limão (m)
lemonade limonada (f)
lens objectiva (f)
 (contact) lente (f)
lentil lentilha (f)
less menos
lesson lição (f)
letter carta (f)
letter box caixa do correio (f)
lettuce alface (f)
library biblioteca (f)
licence licença (f)
 (driving) carta de condução (f)
to lie down deitar-se
lifebelt cinto salva-vidas (m)

lifeboat barco salva-vidas (m)
lifeguard (guarda) salva-vidas (m/f)
life jacket colete salva-vidas (m)
lift (elevator) elevador; ascensor (m)
  (car) boleia (f)
light (lamp) lâmpada; luz (f)
  (colour) claro/a
  to light acender
light bulb lâmpada (f)
lighter isqueiro (m)
to like gostar de
lime lima (f)
lip lábio (m)
lipstick batom (m)
liquid líquido (m)
to listen escutar; ouvir
litre litro (m)
litter lixo (m)
litter-bin caixote de lixo (m)
little pequeno/a
  a little um pouco
to live morar; viver
liver fígado (m)
living room sala de estar (f)
loaf pão (m)
loaf (long) cacete (m)
lobster lagosta (f)
local local
lock fechadura (f)
lollipop chupa-chupa (m)
long comprido; longo/a
loo sanitário (m)/WC
to look olhar
to look after cuidar (de)
to look for procurar
lorry camião (m)
to lose perder
lost property secção de achados e
  perdidos (f)
loud alto/a
lounge sala (de estar) (f)
love amor (m)
  to fall in love apaixonar-se por
  (end of letter) um abraço; um beijo
  to love amar; gostar de
lovely bonito/a
low baixo/a
luggage bagagem (f)

lunch almoço (m)
lunchtime hora do almoço (f)
lung pulmão (m)

M
machine máquina (f)
madam senhora (f)
magazine revista (f)
maid empregada (f)
mail correio (m)
main principal
  main road estrada (f)
to make fazer
make-up maquilhagem (f)
man homem (m)
manager gerente (m/f)
manicure manicura (f)
many muitos/as
map (road) mapa (m)
  (town) planta (f)
margarine margarina (f)
market mercado (m)
marmalade doce de laranja (m)
married casado/a
mascara rímel (m)
Mass Missa (f)
match (for lighting) fósforo (m)
  (sport) partida (f); jogo (m)
material (cloth) tecido (m)
mattress colchão (m)
maybe talvez
mayonnaise maionese (f)
meal refeição (f)
to mean significar; querer dizer
measles sarampo (m)
to measure medir
measurement medida (f)
meat carne (f)
mechanic mecânico/a (m/f)
medicine remédio (m); medicamento (m)
to meet conhecer; encontrar
meeting reunião (f)
melon melão (m)
member membro/a; sócio/a (m/f)
to mend consertar; reparar
menu ementa (f); lista (f)
message recado (m)
meter taxímetro; medidor (m)

metre metro (m)
midday meio-dia (m)
middle meio (m)
midnight meia-noite (f)
mild suave
mile milha (f)
mileage quilometragem (f)
milk leite (m)
milkshake batido de leite (m)
mince carne moída (f)
mineral water água mineral (f)
minimum mínimo (m)
minor menor
 (road) estrada secundária (f)
mint hortelã (f)
minute minuto (m)
mirror espelho (m)
Miss (title) senhora; menina (f)
 to miss (train) perder
missing perdido/a
mistake erro (m)
mistaken errado; enganado/a
mixed salad salada mista (f)
mobile phone telemóvel (m)
moisturising cream creme hidratante (m)
moment momento (m)
monastery monastério (m)
money dinheiro (m)
month mês (m)
monument monumento (m)
moped motorizada (f)
more mais
morning manhã (f)
mosquito mosquito (m)
most maioria (f)
mother mãe (f)
motor motor (m)
motorbike moto (f)
motorist motorista (m/f)
motorway autoestrada (f)
mountain montanha (f)
mouse rato (m)
moustache bigode (m)
mouth boca (f)
to move mexer
 (house) mudar de casa
movie filme (m)
Mr senhor (m)

Mrs senhora (f)
much muito
mug caneca (f)
muscle músculo (m)
museum museu (m)
mushroom cogumelo (m)
music música (f)
musical musical
mussels mexilhões (mpl)
must (to have to) ter de/que; dever
mustard mostarda (f)

N
nail (metal) prego (m)
 (finger) unha (f)
nail file lima (f)
nail polish verniz para as unhas (m)
nail polish remover acetona para as
 unhas (f)
name nome (m)
 surname apelido (m)
napkin guardanapo (m)
nappy fralda (f)
narrow estreito/a
nationality nacionalidade (f)
natural natural
near perto/a
necessary necessário/a
neck pescoço (m)
necklace colar (m)
to need precisar de
needle agulha (f)
neighbour vizinho/a (m/f)
nephew sobrinho (m)
nervous nervoso; ansioso/a
never nunca
new novo/a
news notícias (fpl)
newsagent tabacaria (f)
newspaper jornal (m)
next (in queue) seguinte; próximo/a
 (week etc) próximo/a
next to ao lado de
nice (thing) bonito/bom
 (person) simpático/a
niece sobrinha (f)
night noite (f)
nightclub boite; discoteca (f)

nightdress camisa da noite (f)
no não
noisy barulhento/a
non-alcoholic (drink) sem álcool
non-stop (train) directo/a
normal normal
north norte (m)
Northern Ireland a Irlanda do Norte
nose nariz (m)
nosebleed hemorragia nasal (f)
not não
note (money) nota (f)
 (message) recado (m)
nothing nada
novel romance (m)
now agora/já
nudist nudista (m/f)
nuisance aborrecimento (m); que
 chatice!
number número (m)
number plate matrícula (f)
nurse enfermeiro/a (m/f)
nut (edible) noz (f)

O

object objecto (m)
occupation profissão (f)
off (food etc) passado/a; mau/má
office escritório (m)
often frequentemente
oil óleo (m)
ointment pomada (f)
OK está bem; OK
old velho/a
olive azeitona (f)
olive oil azeite (m)
omelette omeleta (f)
on em; em cima de
one-way (street) (rua) de sentido único (f)
 (ticket) simples; de ida
onion cebola (f)
only só
open aberto/a
 to open abrir
open-air ao ar livre; aberto/a
opera ópera (f)
operation operação (f)
operator (tel) telefonista (m/f)

opposite (place) em frente
optician oculista (m/f)
or ou
orange laranja (f)
orangeade laranjada (f)
orange juice sumo de laranja (m)
orchestra orquestra (f)
to order encomendar; pedir
other outro/a
out of order avariado/a
outside fora
oven forno (m)
over por cima
overdone cozido/a demais
overnight durante a noite
 to stay overnight passar a noite
overseas no estrangeiro
to overtake ultrapassar
to owe dever
owner dono/a (m/f)
oyster ostra (f)

P

package holiday viagem organizada (f)
packet pacote (m)
packet of cigarettes maço de cigarros (m)
pain dor (f)
painkiller analgésico (m)
painting pintura (f)
pair (objects) par (m)
 (people) casal (m)
palace palácio (m)
panties cuecas (fpl)
paper papel (m)
 (journal) jornal (m)
paracetamol parecetamol (m)
parcel embrulho (m); encomenda (f)
pardon? como?
parents pais (mpl)
park parque (m)
 to park estacionar
parking estacionamento (m)
parking meter parquímetro (m)
parking ticket multa (f)
part parte (f)
 (car) peça (f)
partner (social) companheiro; parceiro/a
 (business) sócio/a

party (fun) festa (f)
  (political) partido (m)
passenger passageiro (m)
passport passaporte (m)
path caminho (m)
patient paciente
pavement calçada (f)
to pay pagar
to pay in (at bank) depositar
pea ervilha (f)
peach pêssego (m)
peanut amendoim (m)
pear pêra (f)
pedestrian peão (m)
pedestrian crossing passagem para
  peões (f)
peg (clothes) mola (f)
pen caneta (f)
pencil lápis (m)
penicillin penicilina (f)
penis pénis (m)
pensioner reformado/a (m/f)
people pessoas (fpl)
pepper (condiment) pimenta (f)
  (vegetable) pimentão (m)
per por
performance representação (f)
perfume perfume (m)
perhaps talvez
period período (m)
  (menstrual) menstruação (f)
perm permanente (f)
permit licença (f)
personal pessoal
petrol gasolina (f)
petrol pump bomba de gasolina (f)
petrol station estação (f); posto (m) de
  gasolina
petrol tank depósito (m)
pharmacy farmácia (f)
phone telefone (m)
  to phone telefonar; chamar
phonecard cartão telefónico (m)
photo fotografia (foto) (f)
to pick up ir buscar
picnic piquenique (m)
picture quadro (m)
piece pedaço (m)

pig porco (m)
pill comprimido (m)
  the pill pílula (f)
pillow almofada (f)
pin alfinete (m)
pineapple ananás (m)
pink cor de rosa (f)
pipe (water) cano (m)
  (tobacco) cachimbo (m)
place lugar (m)
plan plano (m)
  (map) planta (f)
plane avião (m)
plant planta (f)
plaster (medical) adesivo (m)
plastic plástico/a
plate prato (m)
platform linha; plataforma (f); cais (m)
play (theatre) peça (f)
  to play brincar
  to play (game) jogar
    (instrument) tocar
playground parque infantil (m)
pleasant agradável
please se faz favor; por favor
plug (sink) tampa (f)
  (electrical) tomada (f)
to plug in ligar
plum ameixa (f)
plumber canalizador/a (m/f)
pocket bolso (m)
poison veneno (m)
police polícia (f)
police station esquadra da polícia (f)
pool (swimming) piscina (f)
poor pobre
popular popular
pork carne de porco (f)
port (harbour) porto (m)
  (drink) vinho do Porto (m)
porter porteiro (m)
portion porção (f)
Portugal Portugal
Portuguese português/portuguesa
possible possível
post correio (m)
  to post enviar; pôr no correio
postage stamp selo (m)

post box caixa de correio (f)
postcard postal (m)
postcode código postal (m)
poster cartaz (m)
postman/woman carteiro/a
post office correios (mpl)
potato batata (f)
pottery (objects) cerâmica (f)
poultry aves (fpl)
pound (weight) libra (f)
 (money) libra (f)
powder pó (m)
pram carrinho de bebé (m)
prawn gamba (f)
precaution precaução (f)
to prefer preferir
pregnant grávida
to prepare preparar
prescription receita (f)
present (gift) prenda (f); presente (m)
press (newspapers) imprensa (f)
 to press (button) carregar
 (trousers) passar
pretty bonito/a
price preço (m)
priest padre (m)
private (personal) pessoal
 (lesson etc) particular
prize prémio (m)
probably provavelmente
problem problema (m)
profession profissão (f)
programme programa (m)
prohibited proibido/a
property propriedade (f)
proprietor proprietário/a; dono/a
to prosecute processar
to protect proteger
pub pub; bar (m)
public público/a
public transport transporte público (m)
to pull puxar
pullover pulover (m)
punch (drink) ponche (m)
 (hit) soco (m)
puncture furo (m)
purple violeta; roxo/a
purse porta-moedas (m)

to push empurrar
pushchair carrinho de bebé (m)
to put pôr

Q
quality qualidade (f)
quantity quantidade (f)
quarter quarto (m)
quay cais (m)
queasy enjoado/a
question pergunta (f)
queue bicha (f)
 to queue fazer bicha
quick rápido/a
quickly rapidamente; depressa
quiet calmo/a
quite bastante

R
rabbit coelho (m)
race (sport) corrida (f)
racket raqueta (f)
radiator radiador (m)
radio rádio (m)
railway caminho de ferro (m)
rain chuva (f)
 to rain chover
raincoat impermeável (m)
rape violação (f)
 to rape violar
rare (meat) mal passado/a
 (unusual) raro/a
rash erupção cutânea (f)
raspberry framboesa (f)
rat ratazana (f)
raw (uncooked) cru/crua
razor navalha (f)
 electric razor aparelho de barbear
  eléctrico (m)
 safety razor aparelho de barbear (m)
 razor blade lâmina de barbear (f)
to reach (arrive) chegar
to read ler
ready pronto/a
real verdadeiro/a
receipt recibo (m)
to receive receber
recent recente

reception (hotel) recepção (f)
receptionist recepcionista (m/f)
to recommend recomendar
record (music) disco (m)
record-player gira-discos (m)
recorded delivery carta registada (f)
to recover recuperar
red encarnado; vermelho/a
refrigerator frigorífico (m)
refund reembolso (m)
to refuse negar
regular regular
relative (family) parente (m)
to relax relaxar
religion religião (m)
to remain ficar; permanecer
to remember lembrar-se
to remove tirar
rent aluguer (m); renda (f)
  to rent alugar
to repair consertar; reparar
to repeat repetir
to replace substituir
to represent representar
representative representante; agente (m/f)
request pedido (m)
  to request pedir
reservation reserva (f)
to reserve reservar
responsible responsável
rest descanso (m)
  to rest descansar
restaurant restaurante (m)
result resultado (m)
retired (person) reformado/a
return (ticket) de ida e volta
to return (go back) voltar
  (money) devolver
reverse (gear) marcha atrás (f)
rib costela (f)
rice arroz (m)
rich rico/a
to ride (horse) andar a cavalo
right (direction) direita (f)
to be right ter razão
rights direitos (mpl)
ring (jewellery) anel (m)

to ring (phone) chamar
  (bell) tocar
ring road circunvalação (f)
ripe maduro/a
risk risco (m)
river rio (m)
road rua; estrada (f)
road sign sinal (m)
roadworks obras (fpl)
roast assado/a
to rob roubar
rock rocha (f)
roll (bread) pãozinho (m)
roof telhado (m)
roof rack porta-bagagem (m)
room (house) quarto (m)
  (hotel) quarto (m)
rope corda (f)
round redondo/a
route caminho (m)
row (theatre) fileira (f)
rubber borracha (f)
rubbish lixo (m)
rucksack mochila (f)
rude malcriado/a
rug tapete (m)
ruins ruínas (fpl)
rules regras (fpl)
to run correr
runway pista de descolagem (f)

S
sad triste
safe (for money) cofre (m)
  (no danger) seguro/a
safety pin alfinete (m)
to sail velejar
sailing boat barco à vela (m)
salad salada (f)
salad cream maionese (f)
salad dressing molho de salada (m)
salami salame (m)
sale venda (f); saldos (mpl)
  for sale vende-se
salesperson vendedor/a (m/f)
salmon salmão (m)
salt sal (m)
same mesmo/a

sand areia (f)
sandal sandália (f)
sandwich sandes (f); sanduíche (m)
sanitary towel penso higiénico (m)
sardine sardinha (f)
sauce molho (m)
saucepan panela (f)
saucer pires (m)
sausage salsicha (f)
to say dizer
scarf cachecol (m)
scenery paisagem (f)
school escola (f)
scissors tesoura (f)
Scotland a Escócia
Scottish escocês/escocesa
screw parafuso (m)
screwdriver chave de parafusos (f)
sea mar (m)
sea food mariscos (mpl)
sea front beira-mar (f)
seaside praia; costa (f)
season estação (f)
season ticket bilhete de temporada (m)
seasoning tempero (m)
seat cadeira (f)
seat belt cinto de segurança (m)
second segundo/a
secretary secretário/a
section secção (f)
to see ver
see you later! até logo!
self-service auto-serviço (m)
to sell vender
to send mandar; enviar
separate separado/a
septic infectado/a
to serve servir
service serviço (m)
serviette guardanapo (m)
several vários/as
to sew costurar
shade sombra (f)
shampoo champô (m)
sharp agudo/a
to shave barbear; fazer a barba
shaver a máquina de barbear (f)
shaving cream/foam creme (m);

espuma (f) de barbear
shawl xaile (m)
sheet (bed) lençol (m)
   (paper) folha (f)
shellfish mariscos (mpl)
sherry xerez (m)
ship barco (m)
shirt camisa (f)
shoe sapato (m)
shoelace atacador (m)
shoe polish pomada de sapatos (f)
shoe repairer's sapateiro (m)
shoe shop sapataria (f)
shop loja (f)
shop assistant vendedor/a; empregado/a
shopping compras (fpl)
   to go shopping ir fazer compras
shopping centre centro comercial (m)
short curto/a
shorts calções (mpl)
short-sighted míope
shoulder ombro (m)
show espectáculo (m)
   to show mostrar
shower duche; chuveiro (m)
shut fechar
sick (ill) doente
   (sea/air) enjoado/a
side effects efeitos colaterais (mpl)
sightseeing turismo (m)
sign sinal (m); placa (f)
   to sign assinar
signature assinatura (f)
silk seda (f)
silly idiota
silver prata (f)
simple simples
since desde
singer cantor/a (m/f)
single (bed, room) (quarto) individual (m)
   (ticket) (bilhete) simples; de ida (m)
   (person) solteiro/a
sink (bathroom) lavatório (m)
sir senhor (m)
sister irmã (f)
size (clothes) tamanho (m); medida (f)
   (shoes) número (m)
   (object) tamanho (m)

ski esqui (m)
  to ski esquiar
skin pele (f)
skirt saia (f)
sky céu (m)
to sleep dormir
sleeping bag saco de dormir (m)
sleeping car carruagem cama (f)
sleeping pill comprimido para dormir (m)
slide (photo) diapositivo (m)
slipper chinelo (m)
slow lento/a
small pequeno/a
small change dinheiro trocado; troco (m)
smell cheiro (m)
to smoke fumar
smoker fumador/a (m/f)
snack refeição ligeira (f)
snack bar café (m)
snorkel tubo de ar (m)
snow neve (f)
soap sabão (m)
socks meias; peúgas (fpl)
soft mole; suave
sole (shoe) sola (f)
  (fish) linguado (m)
some uns/umas
someone alguém
something alguma coisa (f)
sometimes às vezes
somewhere nalgum lugar
son filho (m)
soon logo; já
sore dolorido/a
sore throat dor de garganta (f)
sorry! desculpe!
soup sopa (f)
south sul (m)
souvenir lembrança (f)
spade pá (m)
spanner chave inglesa (f)
spare part peça sobressalente (f)
spare tyre pneu sobressalente (m)
spark-plug vela (f)
to speak falar
special especial
speciality especialidade (f)
speed velocidade (f)

speed limit velocidade máxima (f)
to spell soletrar
to spend gastar
spicy picante
spider aranha (f)
spinach espinafre (m)
spine espinha dorsal (f)
splinter farpa (f)
sponge esponja (f)
  (cake) pão-de-ló (m)
spoon colher (f)
sport desporto (m)
spot (medical) espinha (f)
  (place) lugar (m)
to sprain torcer
spring primavera (f)
square (shape) quadrado/a
  (in town) praça (f); largo (m)
stadium estádio (m)
staff pessoal (m)
stain nódoa (f)
stain remover tiranódoas (m)
stairs escada (f)
stall (theatre) platéia (f)
stamp selo (m)
to start começar
  (car) arrancar; pegar
starter arranque (m)
station estação (f)
stationer's papelaria (f)
to stay ficar; permanecer
steak bife (m); carne de vaca (f)
to steal roubar
steering wheel volante (m)
sterling esterlina
sticking plaster adesivo (m)
stiff neck torcicolo (m)
sting picada (f)
stocking meia (f)
stomach estômago (m)
stop (bus) paragem (f)
  to stop parar
store (small) loja (f)
  (large) armazém (m)
storm tempestade (f)
straight recto; liso/a
straight ahead em frente
straight away imediatamente

straw palha (f)
strawberry morango (m)
stream ribeiro (m)
street rua (f)
student estudante (m/f)
stupid estúpido/a
suburbs arredores (mpl)
suede camurça (f)
sugar açúcar (m)
suit fato (m)
suitcase mala (f)
summer verão (m)
sun sol (m)
to sunbathe tomar sol
sunburn queimadura do sol (f)
sunglasses óculos de sol (mpl)
sunshade pára-sol (m)
sunstroke insolação (f)
sun-tan lotion creme solar (m)
supermarket supermercado (m)
supper jantar (m); ceia (f)
supplement suplemento (m)
suppository supositório (m)
sure seguro/a
surgery (doctor's) consultório (m)
  (operation) cirugia (f)
surname apelido (m)
sweater camisola (f)
sweatshirt camisola de malha (f)
sweet doce
  (dessert) sobremesa (f)
sweet corn milho (m)
sweetener adoçante (m)
sweets rebuçados (mpl)
to swell inchar
to swim nadar
swimming natação (f)
swimming costume fato de banho (m)
swimming pool piscina (f)
swimming trunks calções de banho (mpl)
swing baloiço (m)
switch interruptor (m)
  to switch on acender
  to switch off apagar
swollen inchado/a
symptom sintoma (m)
syrup (medicine) xarope (m)
  (sugar) melaço (m)

T
table mesa (f)
table-cloth toalha de mesa (f)
tablet comprimido (m)
to take tomar; levar
talc pó talco (m)
to talk falar
tall alto/a
tampon tampão (m)
tap torneira (f)
tape fita (f)
tart tarte (f)
tax imposto (m)
tax free isento/a de impostos
tea chá (m)
teaspoon colher de chá (f)
tea towel pano de cozinha (m)
teacher professor/a (m/f)
telegram telegrama (m)
telephone telefone (m)
telephone box cabine telefónica (f)
telephone directory lista telefónica (f)
television televisão (f)
  (set) televisor (m)
to telex mandar um telex
to tell dizer
temperature temperatura (f)
  (fever) febre (f)
tennis ténis (m)
tennis court campo de ténis (m)
tent tenda (f)
terrace terraço (m)
test prova (f)
  (medical) exame (m)
thank you obrigado/a
that esse/a; aquele/a
theft roubo (m)
then então
there ali; lá
thermometer termómetro (m)
these estes/as
thick espesso; grosso/a
thief ladrão (m)
thin fino; magro/a
thing coisa (f)
to think pensar
  (believe) crer; achar
third terceiro/a

to be thirsty ter sede
this este/a
thousand mil
thread fio (m)
throat garganta (f)
through por
  no through road rua sem saída (f)
ticket (train/bus) bilhete (m)
  (cinema) bilhete; entrada (f)
  (shopping) recibo (m)
  (parking) multa (f)
ticket office bilheteira (f)
tide maré (f)
  high tide maré alta (f)
  low tide maré baixa (f)
tie gravata (f)
tights collants (mpl)
time (clock) hora (f)
  (general) tempo (m)
timetable horário (m)
tin (can) lata (f)
tin-opener abre-latas (m)
tip (money) gorjeta (f)
tired cansado/a
tissue lenço de papel (m)
to/towards a; para
toast (bread) torrada (f)
  (cheers) saúde!
tobacco tabaco (m)
tobacconist's tabacaria (f)
today hoje
toe dedo do pé (m)
together juntos/as
toilet lavabo (m); casa de banho (f)
toilet paper papel higiénico (m)
toll portagem (f)
tomato tomate (m)
tomorrow amanhã
tongue língua (f)
tonic water água tónica (f)
tonight esta noite (f)
too também
tooth dente (m)
toothache dor de dentes (f)
toothbrush escova de dentes (f)
toothpaste pasta dentífrica; de dentes (f)
toothpick palito (m)
torch lanterna (f)
total total (m)

tour excursão (f)
tourist turista (m/f)
tourist office Turismo (m)
towel toalha (f)
tower torre (f)
town cidade (f)
town hall câmara municipal (f)
toy brinquedo (m)
tracksuit fato de treino (m)
tractor tractor (m)
traffic trânsito (m)
traffic jam engarrafamento (m)
traffic light semáforo; sinal (m)
traffic warden guarda de trânsito (m/f)
train comboio (m)
transfer (bank) transferência (f)
to translate traduzir
translator tradutor/a (m/f)
to transport transportar
travel viagem (f)
travel agency agência de viagens (f)
traveller's cheques cheques de viagem (mpl)
tray bandeja (f)
tree árvore (f)
trolley carrinho (m)
trousers calças (fpl)
truck camião (m)
to try tentar
T-shirt T-shirt (f)
tuna atum (m)
tunnel túnel (m)
turkey peru (m)
turn (in road) curva (f)
  to turn (a corner) virar; voltar
tweezers pinça (f)
twice duas vezes
type tipo (m)
typical típico/a
tyre pneu (m)

U
ugly feio/a
umbrella guarda-chuva; chapéu de chuva (m)
uncomfortable incómodo/a
unconscious inconsciente; sem sentidos
uncooked crua

under debaixo; em baixo
underdone (meat) mal passado/a
underground metro (m)
underpants cuecas (fpl)
to understand compreender; entender
underwear roupa interior (f)
United States os Estados Unidos
university universidade (f)
unleaded sem chumbo
unmarried solteiro/a
until até
up em cima; para cima
upset (angry) aborrecido/a
upstairs em cima
urgent urgente
to use usar
useful útil
usually geralmente

V

vacancy vaga (f)
vacation férias (fpl)
vaccine vacina (f)
vacuum cleaner aspirador (m)
vacuum flask termo (m)
valley vale (m)
value valor (m)
valuables objectos de valor (mpl)
valve válvula (f)
van carrinha (f)
vanilla baunilha (f)
veal vitela (f)
vegetable legume (m)
vegetarian vegetariano/a
velvet veludo (m)
very muito
vest camisola interior (f)
video machine vídeo (m)
video tape cassette de vídeo (f)
view vista (f)
villa vivenda (f)
village aldeia (f)
vinegar vinagre (m)
visa visto (m)
visit visita (f)
  to visit visitar
visitor visita (f); turista (m/f)
vitamin vitamina (f)
voice voz (f)

voltage voltagem (f)
to vomit vomitar

W

to wait esperar
waiter empregado (m)
waiting room sala de esperar (f)
waitress empregada (f)
to wake (up) acordar-se
Wales o País de Gales
walk passeio (m)
  to walk andar; passear
wall (inside) parede (f)
  (outside) muro (m)
wallet carteira (f)
walnut noz (f)
to want querer
ward (hospital) ala (f)
wardrobe guarda-roupa; armário (m)
warm morno/a; quente
to wash lavar
  to wash the dishes lavar a loiça
washable lavável
wash-basin lavatório (m)
washing machine máquina de lavar
  roupa (f)
washing powder sabão em pó (m)
washing-up liquid detergente para lavar
  loiça (m)
wasp vespa (f)
watch relógio (m)
watch strap pulseira de relógio (f)
water água (f)
waterfall catarata; queda de água (f)
watermelon melancia (f)
water-skiing esqui aquático (m)
watt watt (m)
wave onda (f)
weak fraco/a
weather tempo (m)
weather forecast previsão do tempo (f)
wedding casamento (m)
week semana (f)
weekday dia da semana (m)
weekend fim da semana (m)
to weigh pesar
weight peso (m)
welcome bem vindo/a
well bem

well done bem feito/a
Welsh galês/galesesa
west oeste (m)
wet molhado/a
what que; qual
wheel roda (f)
wheelchair cadeira de rodas (f)
when quando
where onde
which qual
while enquanto
white branco/a
who quem
why porquê
wide largo/a
wife esposa; mulher (f)
to win ganhar
wind vento (m)
window janela (f)
  shop window montra (f)
windscreen pára-brisas (m)
windscreen wiper limpa-pára-brisas (m)
wine vinho (m)
wing asa (f)
winter inverno (m)
with com
without sem
witness testemunha (f)
woman mulher (f)
wood (material) madeira (f)
  (forest) bosque (m)
wool lã (f)
word palavra (f)
work trabalho (m)
  to work (person) trabalhar

  (machine) funcionar
world mundo (m)
to worry preocupar-se
  don't worry! não se preocupe!
wound ferida (f)
to wrap embrulhar
wrapping paper papel de embrulho (m)
wrist pulso (m)
to write escrever
writing paper papel de carta (m)
wrong (mistaken) errado; enganado/a

X
X-ray (department) radiografia (f)
X-rays radiografias (fpl)

y
yacht iate (m)
year ano (m)
yellow amarelo/a
yes sim
yesterday ontem
yet ainda
  (already) já
yoghurt iorgurte (m)
you (informal) tu; você
  (formal) o senhor; a senhora
young jovem
youth hostel albergue (m); pousada (f)
de juventude

Z
zebra crossing passadeira (f)
zip fecho éclair (m)
zoo jardim zoológico (m)

When you get back from your trip, try these **teach yourself** titles, available from all good bookshops and on-line retailers:

- **Teach Yourself One-Day Portuguese**, by Elisabeth Smith
  Only 50 words and phrases to learn with a 75-minute audio CD and an 8-page booklet. Join Andy and Lis on their flight to Portugal and listen in to the 'One-Day Portuguese Challenge'!

- **Teach Yourself Instant Portuguese**, by Elisabeth Smith
  Learn Portuguese in 6 weeks, on a daily diet of 35 minutes. There's a book with audio support on CD or cassette.

Thinking of buying a property in Portugal? You'll need

- **Teach Yourself Buying a Home in Portugal**, by Peter MacBride and Nat MacBride
  The book will help you choose and buy a property abroad, and then will give you the words you'll need to help you restore or maintain it. 90 clearly labelled diagrams and help with the pronunciation on the essential language CD. (Available February 2005.)